THE POET
OF THE WOODS

A COLLECTION
OF POEMS IN ODE TO
THE NIGHTINGALE

By

VARIOUS

WITH AN INTRODUCTORY ESSAY
BY JOHN BURROUGHS

Read & Co.

Copyright © 2021 Ragged Hand

This edition is published by Ragged Hand,
an imprint of Read & Co.

This book is copyright and may not be reproduced or copied in any way without the express permission of the publisher in writing.

British Library Cataloguing-in-Publication Data
A catalogue record for this book is available
from the British Library.

Read & Co. is part of Read Books Ltd.
For more information visit
www.readandcobooks.co.uk

CONTENTS

BIRDS AND POETS
An Essay by John Burroughs..........................9

THE NIGHTINGALE
By W. Swaysland..................................47

THE POET OF THE WOODS

THE NIGHTINGALE
By Sir Philip Sidney...............................53

PHILOMEL
By Richard Barnfield...............................55

TO THE NIGHTINGALE
By William Drummond.............................57

ON THE DEATH OF A NIGHTINGALE
By Thomas Randolph...............................59

SONNET I: TO THE NIGHTINGALE
By John Milton....................................60

LOVE'S NIGHTINGALE
By Richard Crashaw...............................61

TO THE NIGHTINGALE
By Countess of Winchilsea Anne Finch................63

THE NIGHTINGALE
By John Vanbrugh..................................65

THE NIGHTINGALE
By Mark Akenside..................................67

TO THE NIGHTINGALE
By James Thomson.................................70

AN EVENING ADDRESS TO A NIGHTINGALE
By Cuthbert Shaw..................................71

THE NIGHTINGALE AND GLOW-WORM
By William Cowper.................................75

INVOCATION TO THE NIGHTINGALE
By Mary Hays..77

ODE TO THE NIGHTINGALE
By Mary Darby Robinson.............................79

SECOND ODE TO THE NIGHTINGALE
By Mary Darby Robinson.............................83

TO THE NIGHTINGALE
By Ann Radcliffe....................................89

TO THE NIGHTINGALE, WHICH THE
AUTHOR HEARD SING ON NEW YEAR'S DAY
By William Cowper...................................91

TO A NIGHTINGALE
By Charlotte Smith..................................93

ON THE DEPARTURE OF THE NIGHTINGALE
By Charlotte Smith..................................94

THE RETURN OF THE NIGHTINGALE
By Charlotte Smith..................................95

TO THE NIGHTINGALE
By Robert Southey...................................96

THE NIGHTINGALE; A CONVERSATIONAL POEM
By Samuel Taylor Coleridge 97

THE FAIRY, THE ROSE,
AND THE NIGHTINGALE; A FABLE
By Royall Tyler....................................101

O NIGHTINGALE! THOU SURELY ART
By William Wordsworth 103

ODE TO A NIGHTINGALE
By John Keats......................................105

THE NIGHTINGALE
By Horace Smith 110

THE WOODMAN AND THE NIGHTINGALE
By Percy Bysshe Shelley 111

STRADA'S NIGHTINGALE
By William Cowper................................. 115

TO THE NIGHTINGALE
By Charles Tennyson Turner........................ 116

SONG
By Hartley Coleridge............................... 117

THE NIGHTINGALE'S NEST
By John Clare 118

THE NIGHTINGALE; CHILD'S EVENING HYMN
By Felicia Dorothea Hemans........................ 121

TO THE NIGHTINGALE
By John Clare 123

THE NIGHTINGALE
By George Lunt 125

TO THE NIGHTINGALE
By Frances Anne Kemble............................ 127

EASTERN SUNSET
By Frances Anne Kemble............................ 129

TO A NIGHTINGALE
By George Meredith 130

PHILOMELA
By Matthew Arnold................................. 131

TO THE NIGHTINGALE
By Walter Savage Landor 133

CHARADE: 13
By Frances Ridley Havergal......................... 135

APRIL
By John Keble...................................... 136

LYRICAL INTERLUDE: 2
By Heinrich Heine.................................. 139

BIANCA AMONG THE NIGHTINGALES
By Elizabeth Barrett Browning 140

NIGHTINGALES
By Charles Tennyson Turner 143

THE NIGHTINGALE IN THE STUDY
By James Russell Lowell 145

THE NIGHTINGALE'S DEATH SONG
By Felicia Dorothea Hemans 148

THE NIGHTINGALE AND THE ORGAN
By John Godfrey Saxe 150

A NIGHTINGALE IN KENSINGTON GARDENS
By Henry Austin Dobson 153

TEMA CON VARIAZONI: PRELUDE
ByJohn Addington Symonds 155

NIGHTINGALE AND CUCKOO
By Alfred Austin 158

A COLONY OF NIGHTINGALES
By Charles Tennyson Turner 159

NIGHTINGALES IN LINCOLNSHIRE
By Charles Tennyson Turner 161

TO A NIGHTINGALE ON ITS RETURN
By Charles Tennyson Turner 162

THE SICK MAN AND THE NIGHTINGALE
By Amy Levy 163

THE NIGHTINGALE
By Katharine Tynan Hinkson 165

AL FAR DELLA NOTTE
By William Sharp 167

HAST THOU HEARD THE NIGHTINGALE?
By Richard Watson Gilder 169

NIGHTINGALES
By Robert Seymour Bridges 171

MY LOYAL LOVE
By Johanna Ambrosius................................173

TO THE NIGHTINGALE (2)
By William Drummond...............................175

ECHOES: 45
By William Ernest Henley............................176

I. THE ROMANCER (THREE SEVERAL BIRDS)
By James Whitcomb Riley............................177

AN ADDRESS TO THE
NIGHTINGALE (FROM ARISTOPHANES)
By Agnes Mary F. Robinson..........................179

THE NOTIONAL NIGHTINGALE
By Amos Russel Wells................................181

TO THE NIGHTINGALE
By Philip Ayres......................................183

THE NIGHTINGALE THAT WAS DROWNED
By Philip Ayres......................................185

TO A NIGHTINGALE HEARD
UPON A HILLTOP BEFORE DAWN
By Herbert Trench...................................186

A RICHER FREIGHT
By William Henry Davies............................188

NIGHTINGALE LANE
By William Sharp...................................189

THE CHINESE NIGHTINGALE
By Nicholas Vachel Lindsay..........................190

A NIGHTINGALE AT FRESNOY
By Jessie Belle Rittenhouse..........................198

THE SEARCH FOR THE NIGHTINGALE
By Walter James Redfern Turner.....................199

THE SONGSTERS
By William Watson..................................205

FAIRFORD NIGHTINGALES
By John Drinkwater 207

WASTED HOURS
By William Henry Davies 209

THE NIGHTINGALE NEAR THE HOUSE
By Harold Monro................................210

BIBLIOGRAPHY...................................211

BIRDS AND POETS

An Essay by John Burroughs

It might almost be said that the birds are all birds of the poets and of no one else, because it is only the poetical temperament that fully responds to them. So true is this, that all the great ornithologists—original namers and biographers of the birds—have been poets in deed if not in word. Audubon is a notable case in point, who, if he had not the tongue or the pen of the poet, certainly had the eye and ear and heart—"the fluid and attaching character"—and the singleness of purpose, the enthusiasm, the unworldliness, the love, that characterize the true and divine race of bards.

So had Wilson, though perhaps not in as large a measure; yet he took fire as only a poet can. While making a journey on foot to Philadelphia, shortly after landing in this country, he caught sight of the red-headed woodpecker flitting among the trees,—a bird that shows like a tricolored scarf among the foliage,—and it so kindled his enthusiasm that his life was devoted to the pursuit of the birds from that day. It was a lucky hit. Wilson had already set up as a poet in Scotland, and was still fermenting when the bird met his eye and suggested to his soul a new outlet for its enthusiasm.

The very idea of a bird is a symbol and a suggestion to the poet. A bird seems to be at the top of the scale, so vehement and intense is his life,—large-brained, large-lunged, hot, ecstatic, his frame charged with buoyancy and his heart with song. The beautiful vagabonds, endowed with every grace, masters of all climes, and knowing no bounds,—how many human aspirations are realized in their free, holiday lives, and how many suggestions to the poet in their flight and song!

Indeed, is not the bird the original type and teacher of the poet, and do we not demand of the human lark or thrush that he "shake out his carols" in the same free and spontaneous manner as his winged prototype? Kingsley has shown how surely the old minnesingers and early ballad-writers have learned of the birds, taking their key-note from the blackbird, or the wood-lark, or the throstle, and giving utterance to a melody as simple and unstudied. Such things as the following were surely caught from the fields or the woods:—

> "She sat down below a thorn,
> Fine flowers in the valley,
> And there has she her sweet babe borne,
> And the green leaves they grow rarely."

Or the best lyric pieces, how like they are to certain bird-songs!—clear, ringing, ecstatic, and suggesting that challenge and triumph which the outpouring of the male bird contains. (Is not the genuine singing, lyrical quality essentially masculine?) Keats and Shelley, perhaps more notably than any other English poets, have the bird organization and the piercing wild-bird cry. This, of course, is not saying that they are the greatest poets, but that they have preëminently the sharp semi-tones of the sparrows and the larks.

But when the general reader thinks of the birds of the poets, he very naturally calls to mind the renowned birds, the lark and the nightingale, Old World melodists, embalmed in Old World poetry, but occasionally appearing on these shores, transported in the verse of some callow singer.

The very oldest poets, the towering antique bards, seem to make little mention of the song-birds. They loved better the soaring, swooping birds of prey, the eagle, the ominous birds, the vultures, the storks and cranes, or the clamorous sea-birds and the screaming hawks. These suited better the rugged, warlike character of the times and the simple, powerful souls of the singers themselves. Homer must have heard the twittering of the swallows, the cry of the plover, the voice of the turtle, and the warble of the nightingale; but they were not adequate symbols to express what he felt or to adorn his theme. Aeschylus saw in the eagle "the dog of Jove," and his verse cuts like a sword with such a conception.

It is not because the old bards were less as poets, but that they were more as men. To strong, susceptible characters, the music of nature is not confined to sweet sounds. The defiant scream of the hawk circling aloft, the wild whinny of the loon, the whooping of the crane, the booming of the bittern, the vulpine bark of the eagle, the loud trumpeting of the migratory geese sounding down out of the midnight sky; or by the seashore, the coast of New Jersey or Long Island, the wild crooning of the flocks of gulls, repeated, continued by the hour, swirling sharp and shrill, rising and falling like the wind in a storm, as they circle above the beach or dip to the dash of the waves,—are much more welcome in certain moods than any and all mere bird-melodies, in keeping as they are with the shaggy and untamed features of ocean and woods, and suggesting something like the Richard Wagner music in the ornithological orchestra.

> "Nor these alone whose notes
> Nice-fingered art must emulate in vain,
> But cawing rooks, and kites that swim sublime
> In still repeated circles, screaming loud,
> The jay, the pie, and even the boding owl,
> That hails the rising moon, have charms for me,"

says Cowper. "I never hear," says Burns in one of his letters, "the loud, solitary whistle of the curlew in a summer noon, or the wild mixing cadence of a troop of gray plovers in an autumnal morning, without feeling an elevation of soul like the enthusiasm of devotion or poetry."

Even the Greek minor poets, the swarm of them that are represented in the Greek Anthology, rarely make affectionate mention of the birds, except perhaps Sappho, whom Ben Jonson makes speak of the nightingale as—

"The dear glad angel of the spring."

The cicada, the locust, and the grasshopper are often referred to, but rarely by name any of the common birds. That Greek grasshopper must have been a wonderful creature. He was a sacred object in Greece, and is spoken of by the poets as a charming songster. What we would say of birds the Greek said of this favorite insect. When Socrates and Phaedrus came to the fountain shaded by the plane-tree, where they had their famous discourse, Socrates said: "Observe the freshness of the spot, how charming and very delightful it is, and how summer-like and shrill it sounds from the choir of grasshoppers." One of the poets in the Anthology finds a grasshopper struggling in a spider's web, which he releases with the words:—

"Go safe and free with your sweet voice of song."

Another one makes the insect say to a rustic who had captured him:—

"Me, the Nymphs' wayside minstrel whose sweet note
O'er sultry hill is heard, and shady grove to float."

Still another sings how a grasshopper took the place of a broken string on his lyre, and "filled the cadence due."

> "For while six chords beneath my fingers cried,
> He with his tuneful voice the seventh supplied;
> The midday songster of the mountain set
> His pastoral ditty to my canzonet;
> And when he sang, his modulated throat
> Accorded with the lifeless string I smote."

While we are trying to introduce the lark in this country, why not try this Pindaric grasshopper also?

It is to the literary poets and to the minstrels of a softer age that we must look for special mention of the song-birds and for poetical rhapsodies upon them. The nightingale is the most general favorite, and nearly all the more noted English poets have sung her praises. To the melancholy poet she is melancholy, and to the cheerful she is cheerful. Shakespeare in one of his sonnets speaks of her song as mournful, while Martial calls her the "most garrulous" of birds. Milton sang:—

> "Sweet bird, that shunn'st the noise of folly,
> Most musical, most melancholy,
> Thee, chantress, oft the woods among
> I woo, to hear thy evening song."

To Wordsworth she told another story:—

> "O nightingale! thou surely art
> A creature of ebullient heart;
> These notes of thine,—they pierce and pierce,—
> Tumultuous harmony and fierce!
> Thou sing'st as if the god of wine
> Had helped thee to a valentine;
> A song in mockery and despite
> Of shades, and dews, and silent night,
> And steady bliss, and all the loves
> Now sleeping in these peaceful groves."

In a like vein Coleridge sang:—

"'T is the merry nightingale
That crowds and hurries and precipitates
With fast, thick warble his delicious notes."

Keats's poem on the nightingale is doubtless more in the spirit of the bird's strain than any other. It is less a description of the song and more the song itself. Hood called the nightingale

"The sweet and plaintive Sappho of the dell."

I mention the nightingale only to point my remarks upon its American rival, the famous mockingbird of the Southern States, which is also a nightingale,—a night-singer,—and which no doubt excels the Old World bird in the variety and compass of its powers. The two birds belong to totally distinct families, there being no American species which answers to the European nightingale, as there are that answer to the robin, the cuckoo, the blackbird, and numerous others. Philomel has the color, manners, and habits of a thrush,—our hermit thrush,—but it is not a thrush at all, but a warbler. I gather from the books that its song is protracted and full rather than melodious,—a capricious, long-continued warble, doubling and redoubling, rising and falling, issuing from the groves and the great gardens, and associated in the minds of the poets with love and moonlight and the privacy of sequestered walks. All our sympathies and attractions are with the bird, and we do not forget that Arabia and Persia are there back of its song.

Our nightingale has mainly the reputation of the caged bird, and is famed mostly for its powers of mimicry, which are truly wonderful, enabling the bird to exactly reproduce and even improve upon the notes of almost any other songster. But in a state of freedom it has a song of its own which is infinitely rich and various. It is a garrulous polyglot when it chooses to be, and there is a dash of the clown and the buffoon in its nature which too often flavors its whole performance, especially in captivity; but in its native haunts, and when its love-passion is upon it, the serious and even grand side of its character comes out.

In Alabama and Florida its song may be heard all through the sultry summer night, at times low and plaintive, then full and strong.

A friend of Thoreau and a careful observer, who has resided in Florida, tells me that this bird is a much more marvelous singer than it has the credit of being. He describes a habit it has of singing on the wing on moonlight nights, that would be worth going South to hear. Starting from a low bush, it mounts in the air and continues its flight apparently to an altitude of several hundred feet, remaining on the wing a number of minutes, and pouring out its song with the utmost clearness and abandon,—a slowly rising musical rocket that fills the night air with harmonious sounds. Here are both the lark and nightingale in one; and if poets were as plentiful down South as they are in New England, we should have heard of this song long ago, and had it celebrated in appropriate verse. But so far only one Southern poet, Wilde, has accredited the bird this song. This he has done in the following admirable sonnet:—

TO THE MOCKINGBIRD

Winged mimic of the woods! thou motley fool!
    Who shall thy gay buffoonery describe?
Thine ever-ready notes of ridicule
    Pursue thy fellows still with jest and gibe.
Wit—sophist—songster—Yorick of thy tribe,
    Thou sportive satirist of Nature's school,
To thee the palm of scoffing we ascribe,
    Arch scoffer, and mad Abbot of Misrule!
For such thou art by day—but all night long
    Thou pour'st a soft, sweet, pensive, solemn strain,

> As if thou didst in this, thy moonlight song,
> Like to the melancholy Jaques, complain,
> Musing on falsehood, violence, and wrong,
> And sighing for thy motley coat again.

Aside from this sonnet, the mockingbird has got into poetical literature, so far as I know, in only one notable instance, and that in the page of a poet where we would least expect to find him,—a bard who habitually bends his ear only to the musical surge and rhythmus of total nature, and is as little wont to turn aside for any special beauties or points as the most austere of the ancient masters. I refer to Walt Whitman's "Out of the cradle endlessly rocking," in which the mockingbird plays a part. The poet's treatment of the bird is entirely ideal and eminently characteristic. That is to say, it is altogether poetical and not at all ornithological; yet it contains a rendering or free translation of a bird-song—the nocturne of the mockingbird, singing and calling through the night for its lost mate—that I consider quite unmatched in our literature:—

> Once, Paumanok,
> When the snows had melted, and the Fifth-month grass was growing,
> Up this seashore, in some briers,
> Two guests from Alabama—two together,
> And their nest, and four light green eggs, spotted with brown,
> And every day the he-bird, to and fro, near at hand,
> And every day the she-bird, crouched on her nest, silent, with bright eyes,
> And every day I, a curious boy, never too close, never disturbing them,
> Cautiously peering, absorbing, translating.

Shine! Shine! Shine!
Pour down your warmth, great Sun!
While we bask—we two together.

Two together!
Winds blow South, or winds blow North,
Day come white, or night come black,
Home, or rivers and mountains from home,
Singing all time, minding no time,
If we two but keep together.

Till of a sudden,
Maybe killed unknown to her mate,
One forenoon the she-bird crouched not on the nest,
Nor returned that afternoon, nor the next,
Nor ever appeared again.

And thenceforward all summer, in the sound of the sea,
And at night, under the full of the moon, in calmer weather,
Over the hoarse surging of the sea,
Or flitting from brier to brier by day,
I saw, I heard at intervals, the remaining one, the he-bird,
The solitary guest from Alabama.

Blow! blow! blow!
Blow up, sea-winds, along Paumanok's shore!
I wait and I wait, till you blow my mate to me.

Yes, when the stars glistened,
All night long, on the prong of a moss-scalloped stake,
Down, almost amid the slapping waves,
Sat the lone singer, wonderful, causing tears.

He called on his mate:
He poured forth the meanings which I, of all men, know.

Soothe! soothe! soothe!
Close on its wave soothes the wave behind,
And again another behind, embracing and lapping, every one close,
But my love soothes not me, not me.

Low hangs the moon—it rose late.
Oh it is lagging—oh I think it is heavy with love, with love.

Oh madly the sea pushes, pushes upon the land,
With love—with love.

O night! do I not see my love fluttering
out there among the breakers!
What is that little black thing I see there in the white?

Loud! loud! loud!
Loud I call to you, my love!
High and clear I shoot my voice over the waves:
Surely you must know who is here, is here;
You must know who I am, my love.

Low-hanging moon!
What is that dusky spot in your brown yellow?
Oh it is the shape, the shape of my mate!
O moon, do not keep her from me any longer.

Land! land! O land!
Whichever way I turn, oh I think you could give
my mate back again, if you only would;
For I am almost sure I see her dimly whichever way I look.

O rising stars!
Perhaps the one I want so much will rise, will rise with some
of you.

O throat! O trembling throat!
Sound clearer through the atmosphere!
Pierce the woods, the earth;
Somewhere listening to catch you, must be the one I want.

Shake out, carols!
Solitary here—the night's carols!
Carols of lonesome love! Death's carols!
Carols under that lagging, yellow, waning moon!
Oh, under that moon, where she droops almost down into
the sea!
O reckless, despairing carols.

But soft! sink low! Soft! let me just murmur;
And do you wait a moment, you husky-noised sea;
For somewhere I believe I heard my mate responding to me,
So faint—I must be still, be still to listen!
But not altogether still, for then she might
not come immediately to me.

Hither, my love!
Here I am! Here!
With this just-sustained note I announce myself to you;
This gentle call is for you, my love, for you.

Do not be decoyed elsewhere!
That is the whistle of the wind—it is not my voice;
That is the fluttering, the fluttering of the spray;
Those are the shadows of leaves.

O darkness! Oh in vain!
Oh I am very sick and sorrowful.

The bird that occupies the second place to the nightingale in British poetical literature is the skylark, a pastoral bird as the Philomel is an arboreal,—a creature of light and air and motion, the companion of the plowman, the shepherd, the harvester,—whose nest is in the stubble and whose tryst is in the clouds. Its life affords that kind of contrast which the imagination loves,—one moment a plain pedestrian bird, hardly distinguishable from the ground, the next a soaring, untiring songster, reveling in the upper air, challenging the eye to follow him and the ear to separate his notes.

The lark's song is not especially melodious, but is blithesome, sibilant, and unceasing. Its type is the grass, where the bird makes its home, abounding, multitudinous, the notes nearly all alike and all in the same key, but rapid, swarming, prodigal, showering down as thick and fast as drops of rain in a summer shower.

Many noted poets have sung the praises of the lark, or been kindled by his example. Shelley's ode and Wordsworth's "To a Skylark" are well known to all readers of poetry, while every schoolboy will recall Hogg's poem, beginning:—

"Bird of the wilderness,
Blithesome and cumberless,
Sweet be thy matin o'er moorland and lea!
Emblem of happiness,
Blest is thy dwelling-place—
Oh to abide in the desert with thee!"

I heard of an enthusiastic American who went about English fields hunting a lark with Shelley's poem in his hand, thinking no doubt to use it as a kind of guide-book to the intricacies and harmonies of the song.

He reported not having heard any larks, though I have little doubt they were soaring and singing about him all the time, though of course they did not sing to his ear the song that Shelley heard.

The poets are the best natural historians, only you must know how to read them. They translate the facts largely and freely.

A celebrated lady once said to Turner, "I confess I cannot see in nature what you do." "Ah, madam," said the complacent artist, "don't you wish you could!"

Shelley's poem is perhaps better known, and has a higher reputation among literary folk, than Wordsworth's; it is more lyrical and lark-like; but it is needlessly long, though no longer than the lark's song itself, but the lark can't help it, and Shelley can. I quote only a few stanzas:—

> "In the golden lightning
>   Of the sunken sun,
> O'er which clouds are bright'ning
>   Thou dost float and run,
> Like an unbodied joy whose race is just begun.
>
> "The pale purple even
>   Melts around thy flight;
> Like a star of heaven,
>   In the broad daylight
> Thou art unseen, but yet I hear thy shrill delight,
>
> "Keen as are the arrows
>   Of that silver sphere,
> Whose intense lamp narrows
>   In the white dawn clear,
> Until we hardly see—we feel that it is there;

> "All the earth and air
> With thy voice is loud,
> As, when Night is bare,
> From one lonely cloud
> The moon rains out her beams, and Heaven is overflowed."

Wordsworth has written two poems upon the lark, in one of which he calls the bird "pilgrim of the sky." This is the one quoted by Emerson in "Parnassus." Here is the concluding stanza:—

> "Leave to the nightingale her shady wood;
> A privacy of glorious light is thine,
> Whence thou dost pour upon the world a flood
> Of harmony, with instinct more divine;
> Type of the wise, who soar, but never roam,
> True to the kindred points of heaven and home."

The other poem I give entire:—

> "Up with me! up with me into the clouds!
>   For thy song, Lark, is strong;
> Up with me, up with me into the clouds!
>   Singing, singing,
> With clouds and sky about thee ringing,
>   Lift me, guide me till I find
> That spot which seems so to thy mind!
>
> "I have walked through wilderness dreary,
>   And to-day my heart is weary;
> Had I now the wings of a Faery
>   Up to thee would I fly.
> There is madness about thee, and joy divine
>   In that song of thine;
> Lift me, guide me high and high
> To thy banqueting-place in the sky.

> "Joyous as morning
> Thou art laughing and scorning;
> Thou hast a nest for thy love and thy rest,
> And, though little troubled with sloth,
> Drunken Lark! thou wouldst be loth
> To be such a traveler as I.
>   Happy, happy Liver!
> With a soul as strong as a mountain river,
> Pouring out praise to the Almighty Giver,
> Joy and jollity be with us both!
>
> "Alas! my journey, rugged and uneven,
> Through prickly moors or dusty ways must wind;
> But hearing thee, or others of thy kind,
> As full of gladness and as free of heaven,
> I, with my fate contented, will plod on,
> And hope for higher raptures, when life's day is done."

But better than either—better and more than a hundred pages—is Shakespeare's simple line,—

> "Hark, hark, the lark at heaven's gate sings,"

or John Lyly's, his contemporary,—

>   "Who is't now we hear?
> None but the lark so shrill and clear;
> Now at heaven's gate she claps her wings,
> The morn not waking till she sings."

We have no well-known pastoral bird in the Eastern States that answers to the skylark. The American pipit or titlark and the shore lark, both birds of the far north, and seen in the States only in fall and winter, are said to sing on the wing in a similar strain. Common enough in our woods are two birds that have many of the habits and manners of the lark—the water-thrush and the golden-crowned thrush, or oven-bird. They are both walkers, and the latter frequently sings on the wing up aloft after the manner of the lark. Starting from its low perch, it rises in a spiral flight far above the tallest trees, and breaks out in a clear, ringing, ecstatic song, sweeter and more richly modulated than the skylark's, but brief, ceasing almost before you have noticed it; whereas the skylark goes singing away after you have forgotten him and returned to him half a dozen times.

But on the Great Plains, of the West there; is a bird whose song resembles the skylark's quite closely and is said to be not at all inferior. This is Sprague's pipit, sometimes called the Missouri skylark, an excelsior songster, which from far up in the transparent blue rains down its notes for many minutes together. It is, no doubt, destined to figure in the future poetical literature of the West.

Throughout the northern and eastern parts of the Union the lark would find a dangerous rival in the bobolink, a bird that has no European prototype, and no near relatives anywhere, standing quite alone, unique, and, in the qualities of hilarity and musical tintinnabulation, with a song unequaled. He has already a secure place in general literature, having been laureated by no less a poet than Bryant, and invested with a lasting human charm in the sunny page of Irving, and is the only one of our songsters, I believe, that the mockingbird cannot parody or imitate. He affords the most marked example of exuberant pride, and a glad, rollicking, holiday spirit, that can be seen among our birds. Every note expresses complacency and glee. He is a beau of the first pattern, and, unlike any other bird of my acquaintance, pushes his gallantry to the point of wheeling gayly into the train of every female that comes along, even after the season of courtship is over and the matches are all settled; and when she leads him on too wild a chase, he turns, lightly about and breaks out with a song is precisely analogous to a burst of gay and self-satisfied laughter, as much as to say, "Ha!

ha! ha! I must have my fun, Miss Silverthimble, thimble, thimble, if I break every heart in the meadow, see, see, see!"

At the approach of the breeding season the bobolink undergoes a complete change; his form changes, his color changes, his flight changes. From mottled brown or brindle he becomes black and white, earning, in some localities, the shocking name of "skunk bird;" his small, compact form becomes broad and conspicuous, and his ordinary flight is laid aside for a mincing, affected gait, in which he seems to use only the very tips of his wings. It is very noticeable what a contrast he presents to his mate at this season, not only in color but in manners, she being as shy and retiring as he is forward and hilarious. Indeed, she seems disagreeably serious and indisposed to any fun or jollity, scurrying away at his approach, and apparently annoyed at every endearing word and look. It is surprising that all this parade of plumage and tinkling of cymbals should be gone through with and persisted in to please a creature so coldly indifferent as she really seems to be. If Robert O'Lincoln has been stimulated into acquiring this holiday uniform and this musical gift by the approbation of Mrs. Robert, as Darwin, with his sexual selection principle, would have us believe, then there must have been a time when the females of this tribe were not quite so chary of their favors as they are now. Indeed, I never knew a female bird of any kind that did not appear utterly indifferent to the charms of voice and plumage that the male birds are so fond of displaying. But I am inclined to believe that the males think only of themselves and of outshining each other, and not at all of the approbation of their mates, as, in an analogous case in a higher species, it is well known whom the females dress for, and whom they want to kill with envy!

I know of no other song-bird that expresses so much self-consciousness and vanity, and comes so near being an ornithological coxcomb. The red-bird, the yellowbird, the indigo-bird, the oriole, the cardinal grosbeak, and others, all birds of brilliant plumage and musical ability, seem quite unconscious of self, and neither by tone nor act challenge the admiration of the beholder.

By the time the bobolink reaches the Potomac, in September, he has degenerated into a game-bird that is slaughtered by tens of thousands in the marshes. I think the prospects now are of his gradual extermination, as gunners and sportsmen are clearly on the increase, while the limit of the bird's productivity in the North has no doubt been reached long ago. There are no more meadows to be added to his domain there, while he is being waylaid and cut off more and more on his return to the South. It is gourmand eat gourmand, until in half a century more I expect the blithest and merriest of our meadow songsters will have disappeared before the rapacity of human throats.

But the poets have had a shot at him in good time, and have preserved some of his traits. Bryant's poem on this subject does not compare with his lines "To a Water-Fowl,"—a subject so well suited to the peculiar, simple, and deliberate motion of his mind; at the same time it is fit that the poet who sings of "The Planting of the Apple-Tree" should render into words the song of "Robert of Lincoln." I subjoin a few stanzas:—

ROBERT OF LINCOLN

> Merrily swinging on brier and weed,
>   Near to the nest of his little dame,
> Over the mountain-side or mead,
>   Robert of Lincoln is telling his name:
>   Bob-o'-link, bob-o'-link,
>   Spink, spank, spink:
> Snug and safe is that nest of ours,
> Hidden among the summer flowers.
>   Chee, chee, chee.

Robert of Lincoln is gayly drest,
　　Wearing a bright black wedding-coat,
White are his shoulders and white his crest,
　　Hear him call in his merry note:
　　　　Bob-o'-link, bob-o'-link,
　　　　Spink, spank, spink:
Look what a nice new coat is mine,
Sure there was never a bird so fine.
　　　　Chee, chee, chee.

Robert of Lincoln's Quaker wife,
　　Pretty and quiet, with plain brown wings,
Passing at home a patient life,
　　Broods in the grass while her husband sings.
　　　　Bob-o'-link, bob-o'-link,
　　　　Spink, spank, spink:
Brood, kind creature; you need not fear
Thieves and robbers while I am here.
　　　　Chee, chee, chee.

But it has been reserved for a practical ornithologist, Mr. Wilson Flagg, to write by far the best poem on the bobolink that I have yet seen. It is much more in the mood and spirit of the actual song than Bryant's poem:—

THE O'LINCOLN FAMILY

A flock of merry singing-birds were sporting in the grove;
Some were warbling cheerily, and some were making love:
There were Bobolincon, Wadolincon,
Winterseeble, Conquedle,—
A livelier set was never led by tabor, pipe, or fiddle,—
Crying, "Phew, shew, Wadolincon, see, see, Bobolincon,
Down among the tickletops, hiding in the buttercups!
I know the saucy chap, I see his shining cap
Bobbing in the clover there—see, see, see!"

Up flies Bobolincon, perching on an apple-tree,
Startled by his rival's song, quickened by his raillery.
Soon he spies the rogue afloat, curveting in the air,
And merrily he turns about, and warns him to beware!
"'T is you that would a-wooing go, down among the rushes O!
But wait a week, till flowers are cheery,—
wait a week,and, ere you marry,
Be sure of a house wherein to tarry!
Wadolink, Whiskodink, Tom Denny, wait, wait, wait!"

Every one's a funny fellow; every one's a little mellow;
Follow, follow, follow, follow, o'er the hill and in the hollow!
Merrily, merrily, there they hie; now they rise and now they fly;
They cross and turn, and in and out, and down
in the middle, and wheel about,—
With a "Phew, shew, Wadolincon! listen to me, Bobolincon!—
Happy's the wooing that's speedily doing, that's speedily doing,
That's merry and over with the bloom of the clover!
Bobolincon, Wadolincon, Winterseeble, follow, follow me!"

Many persons, I presume, have admired Wordsworth's poem on the cuckoo, without recognizing its truthfulness, or how thoroughly, in the main, the description applies to our own species. If the poem had been written in New England or New York, it could not have suited our case better:—

> "O blithe New-comer! I have heard,
>   I hear thee and rejoice,
> O Cuckoo! shall I call thee Bird,
>   Or but a wandering Voice?
>
> "While I am lying on the grass,
>   Thy twofold shout I hear,
> From hill to hill it seems to pass,
>   At once far off, and near.
>
> "Though babbling only to the Vale,
>   Of sunshine and of flowers,
> Thou bringest unto me a tale
>   Of visionary hours.
>
> "Thrice welcome, darling of the Spring!
>   Even yet thou art to me
> No bird, but an invisible thing,
>   A voice, a mystery;
>
> "The same whom in my schoolboy days
>   I listened to; that Cry
> Which made me look a thousand ways
>   In bush, and tree, and sky.
>
> "To seek thee did I often rove
>   Through woods and on the green;
> And thou wert still a hope, a love;
>   Still longed for, never seen.

> "And I can listen to thee yet;
>   Can lie upon the plain
> And listen, till I do beget
>   That golden time again.
>
> "O blessèd Bird! the earth we pace
>   Again appears to be
> An unsubstantial, faery place;
>   That is fit home for thee!"

Logan's stanzas, "To the Cuckoo," have less merit both as poetry and natural history, but they are older, and doubtless the latter poet benefited by them. Burke admired them so much that, while on a visit to Edinburgh, he sought the author out to compliment him:—

> "Hail, beauteous stranger of the grove!
>   Thou messenger of spring!
> Now Heaven repairs thy rural seat,
>   And woods thy welcome sing.
>
> "What time the daisy decks the green,
>   Thy certain voice we hear;
> Hast thou a star to guide thy path,
>   Or mark the rolling year?

* * * * *

> "The schoolboy, wandering through the wood
>   To pull the primrose gay,
> Starts, the new voice of spring to hear,
>   And imitates thy lay.

* * * * *

"Sweet bird! thy bower is ever green,
　Thy sky is ever clear;
Thou hast no sorrow in thy song,
　No winter in thy year."

The European cuckoo is evidently a much gayer bird than ours, and much more noticeable.

"Hark, how the jolly cuckoos sing
'Cuckoo!' to welcome in the spring,"

says John Lyly three hundred years agone. Its note is easily imitated, and boys will render it so perfectly as to deceive any but the shrewdest ear. An English lady tells me its voice reminds one of children at play, and is full of gayety and happiness. It is a persistent songster, and keeps up its call from morning to night. Indeed, certain parts of Wordsworth's poem—those that refer to the bird as a mystery, a wandering, solitary voice—seem to fit our bird better than the European species. Our cuckoo is in fact a solitary wanderer, repeating its loud, guttural call in the depths of the forest, and well calculated to arrest the attention of a poet like Wordsworth, who was himself a kind of cuckoo, a solitary voice, syllabling the loneliness that broods over streams and woods,—

"And once far off, and near."

Our cuckoo is not a spring bird, being seldom seen or heard in the North before late in May. He is a great devourer of cankerworms, and, when these pests appear, he comes out of his forest seclusion and makes excursions through the orchards stealthily and quietly, regaling himself upon those pulpy, fuzzy titbits. His coat of deep cinnamon brown has a silky gloss and is very beautiful. His note or call is not musical but loud, and has in a remarkable degree the quality of remoteness and introvertedness.

It is like a vocal legend, and to the farmer bodes rain.

It is worthy of note, and illustrates some things said farther back, that birds not strictly denominated songsters, but criers like the cuckoo, have been quite as great favorites with the poets, and have received as affectionate treatment at their hands, as have the song-birds. One readily recalls Emerson's "Titmouse," Trowbridge's "Pewee," Celia Thaxter's "Sandpiper," and others of a like character.

It is also worthy of note that the owl appears to be a greater favorite with the poets than the proud, soaring hawk. The owl is doubtless the more human and picturesque bird; then he belongs to the night and its weird effects. Bird of the silent wing and expansive eye, grimalkin in feathers, feline, mousing, haunting ruins" and towers, and mocking the midnight stillness with thy uncanny cry! The owl is the great bugaboo of the feathered tribes. His appearance by day is hailed by shouts of alarm and derision from nearly every bird that flies, from crows down to sparrows. They swarm about him like flies, and literally mob him back into his dusky retreat. Silence is as the breath of his nostrils to him, and the uproar that greets him when he emerges into the open day seems to alarm and confuse him as it does the pickpocket when everybody cries Thief.

But the poets, I say, have not despised him:—

> "The lark is but a bumpkin fowl;
>   He sleeps in his nest till morn;
> But my blessing upon the jolly owl
>   That all night blows his horn."

Both Shakespeare and Tennyson have made songs about him. This is Shakespeare's, from "Love's Labor's Lost," and perhaps has reference to the white or snowy owl:—

"When icicles hang by the wall,
   And Dick the shepherd blows his nail,
And Tom bears logs into the hall,
   And milk comes frozen home in pail;
When blood is nipped and ways be foul,
Then nightly sings the staring owl,
      Tu-whoo!
Tu-whit! tu-whoo! a merry note,
While greasy Joan doth keel the pot.

"When all aloud the wind doth blow,
   And coughing drowns the parson's saw,
And birds sit brooding in the snow,
   And Marian's nose looks red and raw;
When roasted crabs hiss in the bowl,
Then nightly sings the staring owl,
      Tu-whoo!
Tu-whit! Tu-whoo! a merry note,
While greasy Joan doth keel the pot."

   There is, perhaps, a slight reminiscence of this song in Tennyson's "Owl:"—

"When cats run home and light is come,
   And dew is cold upon the ground,
And the far-off stream is dumb,
   And the whirring sail goes round,
   And the whirring sail goes round;
     Alone and warming his five wits,
     The white owl in the belfry sits.

> "When merry milkmaids click the latch,
> And rarely smells the new-mown hay,
> And the cock hath sung beneath the thatch
> Twice or thrice his roundelay,
> Twice or thrice his roundelay;
> Alone and warming his five wits,
> The white owl in the belfry sits."

Tennyson has not directly celebrated any of the more famous birds, but his poems contain frequent allusions to them. The

> "Wild bird, whose warble, liquid sweet,
> Rings Eden through the budded quicks,
> Oh, tell me where the senses mix,
> Oh, tell me where the passions meet,"

of "In Memoriam," is doubtless the nightingale. And here we have the lark:—

> "Now sings the woodland loud and long,
> And distance takes a lovelier hue,
> And drowned in yonder living blue
> The lark becomes a sightless song."

And again in this from "A Dream of Fair Women:"—

> "Then I heard
> A noise of some one coming through the lawn,
> And singing clearer than the crested bird
> That claps his wings at dawn."

The swallow is a favorite bird with Tennyson, and is frequently mentioned, beside being the principal figure in one of those charming love-songs in "The Princess."

His allusions to the birds, as to any other natural feature, show him to be a careful observer, as when he speaks of

> "The swamp, where hums the dropping snipe."

His single bird-poem, aside from the song I have quoted, is "The Blackbird," the Old World prototype of our robin, as if our bird had doffed the aristocratic black for a more democratic suit on reaching these shores. In curious contrast to the color of its plumage is its beak, which is as yellow as a kernel of Indian corn. The following are the two middle stanzas of the poem:—

> "Yet, though I spared thee all the spring,
>   Thy sole delight is, sitting still,
>   With that gold dagger of thy bill
> To fret the summer jenneting.
>
> "A golden bill! the silver tongue
>   Cold February loved is dry;
>   Plenty corrupts the melody
> That made thee famous once, when young."

Shakespeare, in one of his songs, alludes to the blackbird as the ouzel-cock; indeed, he puts quite a flock of birds in this song:—

> "The ouzel-cock so black of hue,
>   With orange tawny bill;
> The throstle with his note so true,
>   The wren with little quill;
> The finch, the sparrow, and the lark,
>   The plain song cuckoo gray,
> Whose note full many a man doth mark,
>   And dares not answer nay."

So far as external appearances are concerned,—form, plumage, grace of manner,—no one ever had a less promising subject than had Trowbridge in the "Pewee." This bird, if not the plainest dressed, is the most unshapely in the woods. It is stiff and abrupt in its manners and sedentary in its habits, sitting around all day, in the dark recesses of the woods, on the dry twigs and branches, uttering now and then its plaintive cry, and "with many a flirt and flutter" snapping up its insect game.

The pewee belongs to quite a large family of birds, all of whom have strong family traits, and who are not the most peaceable and harmonious of the sylvan folk. They are pugnacious, harsh-voiced, angular in form and movement, with flexible tails and broad, flat, bristling beaks that stand to the face at the angle of a turn-up nose, and most of them wear a black cap pulled well down over their eyes. Their heads are large, neck and legs short, and elbows sharp. The wild Irishman of them all is the great crested flycatcher, a large, leather-colored or sandy-complexioned bird that prowls through the woods, uttering its harsh, uncanny note and waging fierce warfare upon its fellows. The exquisite of the family, and the braggart of the orchard, is the kingbird, a bully that loves to strip the feathers off its more timid neighbors such as the bluebird, that feeds on the stingless bees of the hive, the drones, and earns the reputation of great boldness by teasing large hawks, while it gives a wide berth to little ones.

The best beloved of them all is the phoebe-bird, one of the firstlings of the spring, of whom so many of our poets have made affectionate mention.

The wood pewee is the sweetest voiced, and, notwithstanding the ungracious things I have said of it and of its relations, merits to the full all Trowbridge's pleasant fancies. His poem is indeed a very careful study of the bird and its haunts, and is good poetry as well as good ornithology:—

"The listening Dryads hushed the woods;
   The boughs were thick, and thin and few
   The golden ribbons fluttering through;
Their sun-embroidered, leafy hoods
   The lindens lifted to the blue;
Only a little forest-brook
The farthest hem of silence shook;
When in the hollow shades I heard—
Was it a spirit or a bird?
Or, strayed from Eden, desolate,
Some Peri calling to her mate,
Whom nevermore her mate would cheer?
   'Pe-ri! pe-ri! peer!'

         * * * * *

"To trace it in its green retreat
   I sought among the boughs in vain;
   And followed still the wandering strain,
So melancholy and so sweet,
   The dim-eyed violets yearned with pain.
'T was now a sorrow in the air,
Some nymph's immortalized despair
Haunting the woods and waterfalls;
And now, at long, sad intervals,
Sitting unseen in dusky shade,
His plaintive pipe some fairy played,
With long-drawn cadence thin and clear,—
   'Pe-wee! pe-wee! peer!'

"Long-drawn and clear its closes were—
   As if the hand of Music through
   The sombre robe of Silence drew
A thread of golden gossamer;
   So pure a flute the fairy blew.
Like beggared princes of the wood,
In silver rags the birches stood;
The hemlocks, lordly counselors,
Were dumb; the sturdy servitors,
In beechen jackets patched and gray,
Seemed waiting spellbound all the day
That low, entrancing note to hear,—
   'Pe-wee! pe-wee! peer!'

"I quit the search, and sat me down
   Beside the brook, irresolute,
   And watched a little bird in suit
Of sober olive, soft and brown,
   Perched in the maple branches, mute;
With greenish gold its vest was fringed,
Its tiny cap was ebon-tinged,
With ivory pale its wings were barred,
And its dark eyes were tender-starred.
"Dear bird," I said, "what is thy name?"
And thrice the mournful answer came,
So faint and far, and yet so near,—
   'Pe-wee! pe-wee! peer!'

"For so I found my forest bird,—
  The pewee of the loneliest woods,
  Sole singer in these solitudes,
Which never robin's whistle stirred,
  Where never bluebird's plume intrudes.
Quick darting through the dewy morn,
The redstart trilled his twittering horn
And vanished in thick boughs; at even,
Like liquid pearls fresh showered from heaven,
The high notes of the lone wood thrush
Fell on the forest's holy hush;
But thou all day complainest here,—
  'Pe-wee! pe-wee! peer!'"

 Emerson's best natural history poem is the "Humble-Bee,"—a poem as good in its way as Burns's poem on the mouse; but his later poem, "The Titmouse," has many of the same qualities, and cannot fail to be acceptable to both poet and naturalist.

 The chickadee is indeed a truly Emersonian bird, and the poet shows him to be both a hero and a philosopher. Hardy, active, social, a winter bird no less than a summer, a defier of both frost and heat, lover of the pine-tree, and diligent searcher after truth in the shape of eggs and larvae of insects, preëminently a New England bird, clad in black and ashen gray, with a note the most cheering and reassuring to be heard in our January woods,—I know of none other of our birds so well calculated to captivate the Emersonian muse.

 Emerson himself is a northern hyperborean genius,—a winter bird with a clear, saucy, cheery call, and not a passionate summer songster. His lines have little melody to the ear, but they have the vigor and distinctness of all pure and compact things. They are like the needles of the pine—"the snow loving pine"— more than the emotional foliage of the deciduous trees, and the titmouse becomes them well:—

"Up and away for life! be fleet!—
The frost-king ties my fumbling feet,
Sings in my ears, my hands are stones,
Curdles the blood to the marble bones,
Tugs at the heart-strings, numbs the sense,
And hems in life with narrowing fence.
Well, in this broad bed lie and sleep,—
The punctual stars will vigil keep,—
Embalmed by purifying cold;
The wind shall sing their dead march old,
The snow is no ignoble shroud,
The moon thy mourner, and the cloud.

"Softly,—but this way fate was pointing,
'T was coming fast to such anointing,
When piped a tiny voice hard by,
Gay and polite, a cheerful cry,
Chick-chickadeedee! saucy note,
Out of sound heart and merry throat,
As if it said 'Good day, good sir!
Fine afternoon, old passenger!
Happy to meet you in these places,
Where January brings few faces.'

"This poet, though he lived apart,
Moved by his hospitable heart,
Sped, when I passed his sylvan fort,
To do the honors of his court,
As fits a feathered lord of land;
Flew near, with soft wing grazed my hands
Hopped on the bough, then darting low,
Prints his small impress on the snow,
Shows feats of his gymnastic play,
Head downward, clinging to the spray.

"Here was this atom in full breath,
Hurling defiance at vast death;
This scrap of valor just for play
Fronts the north-wind in waistcoat gray,
As if to shame my weak behavior;
I greeted loud my little savior,
'You pet! what dost here? and what for?
In these woods, thy small Labrador,
At this pinch, wee San Salvador!
What fire burns in that little chest,
So frolic, stout, and self-possest?
Henceforth I wear no stripe but thine;
Ashes and jet all hues outshine.
Why are not diamonds black and gray,
To ape thy dare-devil array?
And I affirm, the spacious North
Exists to draw thy virtue forth.
I think no virtue goes with size;
The reason of all cowardice
Is, that men are overgrown,
And, to be valiant, must come down
To the titmouse dimension.'

* * * * *

"I think old Caesar must have heard
In northern Gaul my dauntless bird,
And, echoed in some frosty wold,
Borrowed thy battle-numbers bold.
And I will write our annals new
And thank thee for a better clew.
I, who dreamed not when I came here
To find the antidote of fear,
Now hear thee say in Roman key,
Poean! Veni, vidi, vici."

A late bird-poem, and a good one of its kind, is Celia Thaxter's "Sandpiper," which recalls Bryant's "Water-Fowl" in its successful rendering of the spirit and atmosphere of the scene, and the distinctness with which the lone bird, flitting along the beach, is brought before the mind. It is a woman's or a feminine poem, as Bryant's is characteristically a man's.

The sentiment or feeling awakened by any of the aquatic fowls is preëminently one of loneliness. The wood duck which your approach starts from the pond or the marsh, the loon neighing down out of the April sky, the wild goose, the curlew, the stork, the bittern, the sandpiper, awaken quite a different train of emotions from those awakened by the land-birds. They all have clinging to them some reminiscence and suggestion of the sea. Their cries echo its wildness and desolation; their wings are the shape of its billows.

Of the sandpipers there are many varieties, found upon the coast and penetrating inland along the rivers and water-courses, one of the most interesting of the family, commonly called the "tip-up," going up all the mountain brooks and breeding in the sand along their banks; but the characteristics are the same in all, and the eye detects little difference except in size.

The walker on the beach sees it running or flitting before him, following up the breakers and picking up the aquatic insects left on the sands; and the trout-fisher along the farthest inland stream likewise intrudes upon its privacy. Flitting along from stone to stone seeking its food, the hind part of its body "teetering" up and down, its soft gray color blending it with the pebbles and the rocks, or else skimming up or down the stream on its long, convex wings, uttering its shrill cry, the sandpiper is not a bird of the sea merely; and Mrs. Thaxter's poem is as much for the dweller inland as for the dweller upon the coast:—

THE SANDPIPER

Across the narrow beach we flit,
   One little sandpiper and I;
And fast I gather, bit by bit,
   The scattered driftwood bleached and dry.
The wild waves reach their hands for it,
   The wild wind raves, the tide runs high,
As up and down the beach we flit,—
   One little sandpiper and I.

Above our heads the sullen clouds
   Scud black and swift across the sky;
Like silent ghosts in misty shrouds
   Stand out the white lighthouses high.
Almost as far as eye can reach
   I see the close-reefed vessels fly,
As fast we flit along the beach,—
   One little sandpiper and I.

I watch him as he skims along,
   Uttering his sweet and mournful cry;
He starts not at my fitful song,
   Or flash of fluttering drapery;
He has no thought of any wrong;
   He scans me with a fearless eye.
Stanch friends are we, well tried and strong,
   The little sandpiper and I.

Comrade, where wilt thou be to-night
   When the loosed storm breaks furiously?
My driftwood fire will burn so bright!
   To what warm shelter canst thou fly?
I do not fear for thee, though wroth
   The tempest rushes through the sky;

> For are we not God's children both,
> Thou, little sandpiper, and I?

Others of our birds have been game for the poetic muse, but in most cases the poets have had some moral or pretty conceit to convey, and have not loved the bird first. Mr. Lathrop preaches a little in his pleasant poem, "The Sparrow," but he must some time have looked upon the bird with genuine emotion to have written the first two stanzas:—

> "Glimmers gay the leafless thicket
> Close beside my garden gate,
> Where, so light, from post to wicket,
> Hops the sparrow, blithe, sedate:
> Who, with meekly folded wing,
> Comes to sun himself and sing.
>
> "It was there, perhaps, last year,
> That his little house he built;
> For he seems to perk and peer,
> And to twitter, too, and tilt
> The bare branches in between,
> With a fond, familiar mien."

The bluebird has not been overlooked, and Halleek, Longfellow, and Mrs. Sigourney have written poems upon him, but from none of them does there fall that first note of his in early spring,—a note that may be called the violet of sound, and as welcome to the ear, heard above the cold, damp earth; as is its floral type to the eye a few weeks later Lowell's two lines come nearer the mark:—

> "The bluebird, shifting his light load of song
> From post to post along the cheerless fence."

Or the first swallow that comes twittering up the southern valley, laughing a gleeful, childish laugh, and awakening such memories in the heart, who has put him in a poem? So the hummingbird, too, escapes through the finest meshes of rhyme.

The most melodious of our songsters, the wood thrush and the hermit thrush,—birds whose strains, more than any others, express harmony and serenity,—have not yet, that I am aware, had reared to them their merited poetic monument, unless, indeed, Whitman has done this service for the hermit thrush in his "President Lincoln's Burial Hymn." Here the threnody is blent of three chords, the blossoming lilac, the evening star, and the hermit thrush, the latter playing the most prominent part throughout the composition. It is the exalting and spiritual utterance of the "solitary singer" that calms and consoles the poet when the powerful shock of the President's assassination comes upon him, and he flees from the stifling atmosphere and offensive lights and conversation of the house,—

"Forth to hiding, receiving night that talks not,
Down to the shores of the water, the path by the swamp in the dimness,
To the solemn shadowy cedars and ghostly pines so still."

Numerous others of our birds would seem to challenge attention by their calls and notes. There is the Maryland yellowthroat, for instance, standing in the door of his bushy tent, and calling out as you approach, *"which way, sir! which way, sir!"* If he says this to the ear of common folk, what would he not say to the poet? One of the peewees says *"stay there!"* with great emphasis. The cardinal grosbeak calls out *"what cheer" "what cheer;"* " the bluebird says *"purity," "purity," "purity;"* the brown thrasher, or ferruginous thrush, according to Thoreau, calls out to the farmer planting his corn, *"drop it," "drop it," "cover it up," "cover it up"* The yellow-breasted chat says *"who,"* *"who"* and *"tea-boy"* What the robin says, caroling that simple strain from the top of the tall maple, or the crow with his hardy haw-haw, or the pedestrain meadowlark sounding his piercing and long-drawn note in the spring meadows, the poets ought to be able to tell us. I only know the birds all have a language which is very expressive, and which is easily translatable into the human tongue.

An Essay from
Birds and Poets, 1877

THE NIGHTINGALE

By W. Swaysland

Sylvia luscinia.
Motacilla " "
Philomela " "

NO bird has had so many tributes paid to it, both by poets and prose writers, as this altogether unequalled songster. Its voice is unrivalled. The Blackcap, Lark, Blackbird, Thrush, and Robin, all fail to approach this " Queen of Song."

Yet few who have read of the wonderful power of voice that belongs to the Nightingales may have had the exquisite pleasure of hearing one of their delicious vocal contests; for it is when, in a still June night, Nightingale answers to Nightingale, and all the power of their combination of sweet sounds is put forth, that the entrancing influence of the song of the Nightingale is most deeply felt. Once heard, it is never forgotten, be it the plaintive long-drawn-out "Wheet, wheet, wheet!" or the mellow "Jug, jug, jug!" or any of the other numerous and not-to-be-described phrases contained in the repertory of this beautiful singer.

Although possessing so sweet a voice, the plumage of the Nightingale is very plain, although its form is graceful. The whole upper part of the bird is rich chestnut-brown, slightly brighter upon the wings ; the tail, which is rather long and rounded, is of a reddish-brown; the breast is dull whitish-grey, somewhat tinged with brown; the throat and under part are pale whitish-grey.

The female is with difficulty distinguished from the male, although she may possibly be smaller, and her eye not quite so large and bold. Some say that her throat is lighter.

The young birds are clad in somewhat similar plumage to young Robins, inasmuch as the brown is lighter than that of the adult birds, and the feathers being tipped with buff they have a mottled appearance.

The Nightingale arrives in England about the early part of April, the males preceding the females by about a week, or, at times, even a fortnight. As a rule they fly to their old retreats, although at times they will desert them, even for years, and then return again in augmented numbers. At this time the males continually sing, possibly with the intention of attracting a mate.

The usual haunts of the Nightingale are groves, small shady copses, plantations, woods, quiet gardens, and thick hedgerows, especially where a little thicket has been allowed to grow; and from these retreats, more particularly whilst building the nest, the beautiful song of the Nightingale is delivered both by day and night.

The nest is placed in a hollow of the ground, or in the roots or stump of a tree, or towards the bottom of a hedgerow. It is built of various materials, including leaves, dry grass-stalks, and bits of bark and fibrous roots, loosely constructed, but lined with finer grasses and horse-hair.

The eggs are generally five in number, and of an olive green colour.

The food of the Nightingale is almost entirely insectivorous, as it comprises such insects as caterpillars, beetles, moths and flies, small worms, and the larvae of ants. Some birds also eat fruit, such as elderberries and currants.

The food of the young whilst in the nest is principally composed of small green caterpillars and worms.

Although Nightingales affect certain districts, where many pairs may be found, they notwithstanding keep almost strictly in pairs ; and if by chance they meet, they will invariably fight, after the manner of Robins. Even the spirit of their song is at times uttered as if in a tone of acute rivalry, though as a rule it is one impassioned love story, poured out on behalf of the mate who is so patiently attending to the duties of incubation.

Before leaving England, which happens in July and August, both the young and adult birds moult, but the young ones only partially, as they retain their wing and tail feathers. The song, too, of the adult bird ceases in a great degree some time in June, as soon as the nesting operations are over; yet these latter are often delayed if the first nest is taken or destroyed. The call-note of the bird is varied, sometimes being "Purr, purr!" and again a sort of "Wheet!" uttered somewhat sharply.

The flight is somewhat short, though also capable of much further extension; and is generally from bush to bush, as these birds seldom stray from their usual haunts.

The migration is usually at night, which peculiarity may account in a great degree for their nocturnal singing, especially as the males would thereby attract the later arriving females.

Some naturalists have gone so far as to imagine that the day-singers were distinct from the nocturnal ones, and others that the parent birds took turns in sitting upon the eggs, and that it was the female whose voice so enchanted their ears in the stillness of evening; but both these ideas are now exploded.

A CHAPTER FROM
Familiar Wild Birds, 1883

THE POET OF THE WOODS

A COLLECTION
OF POEMS IN ODE TO
THE NIGHTINGALE

THE NIGHTINGALE

By Sir Philip Sidney

To the Tune of
"Non Credo Gia Che Piu Infelice Amante"

The nightingale, as soon as April bringeth
   Unto her rested sense a perfect waking,
While late bare earth, proud of new clothing, springeth,
   Sings out her woes, a thorn her song-book making,
   And mournfully bewailing,
Her throat in tunes expresseth
What grief her breast oppresseth
   For Tereus' force on her chaste will prevailing.
O Philomela fair, O take some gladness,
That here is juster cause of plaintful sadness:
Thine earth now springs, mine fadeth;
Thy thorn without, my thorn my heart invadeth.

II

    Alas, she hath no other cause of anguish
But Tereus' love, on her by strong hand wroken,
      Wherein she suffering, all her spirits languish;
Full womanlike complains her will was broken.
    But I, who daily craving,
Cannot have to content me,
Have more cause to lament me,
      Since wanting is more woe than too much having.
O Philomela fair, O take some gladness,
That here is juster cause of plaintful sadness:
Thine earth now springs, mine fadeth;
Thy thorn without, my thorn my heart invadeth.

PHILOMEL

By Richard Barnfield

As it fell upon a day
In the merry month of May,
Sitting in a pleasant shade
Which a grove of myrtles made,
Beasts did leap and birds did sing,
Trees did grow and plants did spring;
Everything did banish moan
Save the Nightingale alone:
She, poor bird, as all forlorn
Leaned her breast up-till a thorn,
And there sung the doleful'st ditty,
That to hear it was great pity.
Fie, fie, fie! now would she cry;
Tereu, Tereu! by and by;
That to hear her so complain
Scarce I could from tears refrain;
For her griefs so lively shown
Made me think upon mine own.
Ah! thought I, thou mourn'st in vain,
None takes pity on thy pain:
Senseless trees they cannot hear thee,
Ruthless beasts they will not cheer thee:
King Pandion he is dead,
All thy friends are lapped in lead;
All thy fellow birds do sing
Careless of thy sorrowing:

Even so, poor bird, like thee,
None alive will pity me.
Whilst as fickle Fortune smiled,
Thou and I were both beguiled,
Every one that flatters thee
Is no friend in misery.
Words are easy, like the wind;
Faithful friends are hard to find:
Every man will be thy friend
Whilst thou hast wherewith to spend;
But if store of crowns be scant,
No man will supply thy want.
If that one be prodigal,
Bountiful they will him call,
And with such-like flattering,
" Pity but he were a king;"
If he be addict to vice,
Quickly him they will entice;
If to women he be bent,
They have at commandment:
But if Fortune once do frown,
Then farewell his great renown;
They that fawn'd on him before
Use his company no more.
He that is thy friend indeed,
He will help thee in thy need:
If thou sorrow, he will weep;
If thou wake, he cannot sleep;
Thus of every grief in heart
He with thee doth bear a part.
These are certain signs to know
Faithful friend from flattering foe.

TO THE NIGHTINGALE

By William Drummond

Sweet bird, that sing'st away the early hours
Of winters past or coming, void of care,
Well pleased with delights which present are,
Fair seasons, budding sprays, sweet-smelling flow'rs:
To rocks, to springs, to rills, from leafy bow'rs
Thou thy Creator's goodness dost declare,
And what dear gifts on thee He did not spare:
A stain to human sense in sin that low'rs.
What soul can be so sick which by thy songs
(Attir'd in sweetness) sweetly is not driven
Quite to forget earth's turmoils, spites, and wrongs,
And lift a reverend eye and thought to heaven?
   Sweet artless songster, thou my mind dost raise
   To airs of spheres, yes, and to angels' lays.

THE POET OF THE WOODS

ON THE DEATH OF A NIGHTINGALE

By Thomas Randolph

GOe solitary wood, and henceforth be
Acquainted with no other Harmonie,
Then the Pyes chattering, or the shrieking note
Of bodeing Owles, and fatall Ravens throate.
Thy sweetest Chanters dead, that warbled forth
Layes, that might tempests calme, and still the North;
And call downe Angels from their glorious Spheare
To heare her Songs, and learne new Anthems there.
That soule is fled, and to *Elisium* gone;
Thou a poore desert left; goe then and runne,
Begge there to stand a grove, and if shee please
To sing againe beneath thy shadowy Trees;
The soules of happy Lovers crown'd with blisses
Shall flock about thee, and keepe time with kisses.

SONNET I:
TO THE NIGHTINGALE

By John Milton

O Nightingale, that on yon bloomy Spray
   Warbl'st at eeve, when all the Woods are still,
   Thou with fresh hope the Lovers heart dost fill,
   While the jolly hours lead on propitious May,
Thy liquid notes that close the eye of Day,
   First heard before the shallow Cuccoo's bill
   Portend success in love; O if Jove's will
   Have linkt that amorous power to thy soft lay,
Now timely sing, ere the rude Bird of Hate
   Foretell my hopeles doom in som Grove ny:
     As thou from yeer to yeer hast sung too late
For my relief, yet hadst no reason why,
   Whether the Muse, or Love call thee his mate,
   Both them I serve, and of their train am I.

LOVE'S NIGHTINGALE

By Richard Crashaw

Though now 'tis neither May nor June
And Nightingales are out of tune,
Yett in these leaves (Faire one) there lyes
(Sworne servant to your sweetest Eyes)
A Nightingale, who may shee spread
In your white bosome her chast bed,
Spite of all the Maiden snow
Those pure untroden pathes can show,
You streight shall see her wake and rise
Taking fresh Life from your fayre Eyes;
And with clasp't winges proclayme a spring
Where Love and shee shall sit and sing,
For lodg'd so ne're your sweetest throte
What Nightingale can loose her noate?
Nor lett her kinred birds complayne
Because shee breakes the yeares old raigne,
For lett them know shee's none of those
Hedge-Quiristers whose Musicke owes
Onely such straynes as serve to keepe
Sad shades and sing dull Night asleepe.
No shee's a Priestesse of that Grove
The holy chappell of chast Love
Your Virgin bosome. Then what e're
Poore Lawes divide the publicke yeare,
Whose revolutions wait upon
The wild turnes of the wanton sun;

Bee you the Lady of Loves Yeere:
Where your Eyes shine his suns appeare:
There all the yeare is Loves long spring.
   There all the yeare
Loves Nightingales shall sitt and sing.

TO THE NIGHTINGALE

By Countess of Winchilsea Anne Finch

Exert thy voice, sweet harbinger of spring!
    This moment is thy time to sing,
    This moment I attend to praise,
And set my numbers to they lays.
    Free as thine shall be my song;
    As they music, short, or long.
Poets, wild as thee, were born,
    Pleasing best when unconfined,
    When to please is least designed,
Soothing but their cares to rest;
    Cares do still their thoughts molest,
    And still th' unhappy poet's breast,
Like thine, when best he sings, is placed against a thorn.

She begins, Let all be still!
    Muse, they promise now fulfill!
Sweet, oh! sweet, still sweeter yet
Can thy words such accents fit,
Canst thou syllables refine,
Melt a sense that shall retain
Still some spirit of the brain,
Till with sounds like these it join.
    'Twill not be! then change thy note;
    Let division shake thy throat.
Hark! Division now she tries;
Yet as far the Muse outflies.

    Cease then, prithee, cease thy tune;
    Trifler, wilt thou sing till *June*?
Till thy business all lies waste,
And the time of building's past!
    Thus we poets that have speech,
Unlike what they forests teach,
    If a fluent vein be shown
    That's transcendant to our own,
Criticize, reform, or preach,
Or censure what we cannot reach.

THE NIGHTINGALE

By John Vanbrugh

ONCE on a time a nightingale
   To changes prone;
Unconstant, fickle, whimsical,
   (A female one)
Who sang like others of her kind,
   Hearing a well-taught linnet's airs,
Had other matters in her mind,
   To imitate him she prepares.
Her fancy straight was on the wing:
   "I fly," quoth she,
"As well as he;
   I don't know why
   I should not try
As well as he to sing."
From that day forth she changed her note,
She spoiled her voice, she strained her throat:
She did, as learned women do,
   Till everything
   That heard her sing,
Would run away from her — as I from you.

THE POET OF THE WOODS

THE NIGHTINGALE

By Mark Akenside

To-night retired, the queen of heaven
  With young Endymion stays;
And now to Hesper it is given
Awhile to rule the vacant sky,
Till she shall to her lamp supply
  A stream of brighter rays.

Propitious send thy golden ray,
  Thou purest light above!
Let no false flame seduce to stray
Where gulf or steep lie hid for harm;
But lead where music's healing charm
  May soothe afflicted love.

To them, by many a grateful song
  In happier seasons vow'd,
These lawns, Olympia's haunts, belong:
Oft by yon silver stream we walk'd,
Or fix'd, while Philomela talk'd,
  Beneath yon copses stood.

THE POET OF THE WOODS

Nor seldom, where the beechen boughs
    That roofless tower invade,
We came, while her enchanting Muse
The radiant moon above us held:
Till, by a clamorous owl compell'd,
    She fled the solemn shade.

But hark! I hear her liquid tone!
    Now Hesper guide my feet!
Down the red marl with moss o'ergrown,
Through yon wild thicket next the plain,
Whose hawthorns choke the winding lane
    Which leads to her retreat.

See the green space: on either hand
    Enlarged it spreads around:
See, in the midst she takes her stand,
Where one old oak his awful shade
Extends o'er half the level mead,
    Enclosed in woods profound.

Hark! how through many a melting note
    She now prolongs her lays:
How sweetly down the void they float!
The breeze their magic path attends;
The stars shine out; the forest bends;
    The wakeful heifers graze.

Whoe'er thou art whom chance may bring
    To this sequester'd spot,
If then the plaintive Siren sing,
O softly tread beneath her bower
And think of Heaven's disposing power,
    Of man's uncertain lot.

THE POET OF THE WOODS

O think, o'er all this mortal stage
  What mournful scenes arise:
What ruin waits on kingly rage;
How often virtue dwells with woe;
How many griefs from knowledge flow;
  How swiftly pleasure flies!

O sacred bird! let me at eve,
  Thus wandering all alone,
Thy tender counsel oft receive,
Bear witness to thy pensive airs,
And pity Nature's common cares,
  Till I forget my own.

TO THE NIGHTINGALE

By James Thomson

O nightingale, best poet of the grove,
   That plaintive strain can ne'er belong to thee,
Blessed in the full possession of thy love:
   O lend that strain, sweet Nighingale, to me!

'Tis mine, alas! to mourn a wretched fate:
   I love a maid who all my bosom charms,
Yet lose my days without this lovely mate;
   Inhuman fortune keeps her from my arms.

You happy birds! by nature's simple laws
   Lead your soft lives, sustained by nature's fare;
You dwell wherever roving fancy draws,
   And love and song is all your pleasing care:

But we, vain slaves of interest and of pride,
   Dare not be blessed, lest envious tongues should blame;
And hence, in vain I languish for my bride!
   O mourn with me, sweet bird, my hapless flame.

AN EVENING ADDRESS TO A NIGHTINGALE

By Cuthbert Shaw

SWEET bird! that, kindly perching near,
Pourest thy plaints melodious in mine ear,
Not, like base worldlings, tutor'd to forego
The melancholy haunts of woe,
   Thanks for thy sorrow-soothing strain:
For surely thou hast known to prove,
Like me, the pangs of hapless love,
   Else why so feelingly complain,
And with thy piteous notes thus sadden all the grove?

Say, dost thou mourn thy ravish'd mate,
   That oft enamour'd on thy strains has hung?
Or has the cruel hand of fate
   Bereft thee of thy darling young?
               Alas! for *both* I weep
In all the pride of youthful charms,
A beauteous bride torn from my circling arms!
A lovely babe that should have liv'd to bless,
   And fill my doating eyes with frequent tears,
At once the source of rapture and distress,
   The flattering prop of my declining years!
In vain from death to rescue I essay'd,
   By every art that science could devise,
Alas! it languished for a mother's aid,

And wing'd its flight to seek her in the skies
Then, O, our comforts be the same
   At evening's peaceful hour,
To shun the noisy paths of wealth and fame,
   And breathe our sorrows in this lonely bower.

But why, alas ! to thee complain?
To thee unconscious of my pain!
Soon shalt thou cease to mourn thy lot severe,
And hail the dawning of a happier year:
The genial warmth of joy-renewing spring
     Again shall plume thy shatter'd wing;
     Again thy little heart shall transport prove,
     Again shall flow thy notes responsive to thy love:
But O for me in vain may seasons roll,
   Nought can dry up the fountain of my tears,
Deploring still the *comfort of my soul,*
   I court my sorrows by increasing years.

Tell me, thou syren hope, deceiver, say,
   Where is the promis'd period of my woes?
Full three long lingering years have roll'd away,
   And yet I weep, a stranger to repose:
     O what delusion did thy tongue employ!
"That *Emma's* fatal pledge of love,
   Her last bequest with all a mother's care,
The bitterness of sorrow should remove,
   Soften the horrors of despair,
     And cheer a heart long lost to joy!"
How oft, when fondling in mine arjns,
   Gazing enraptur'd on its angel face,
   My soul the maze of fate would vainly trace,
And burn with all a father's fond alarms!
And O what flattering scenes had fancy feign'd!
How did 1 rave of blessings yet in store!

Till every aching sense was sweetly pain'd,
  And my full heart could bear, nor tongue could utter more.

"Just Heaven," I cried, with recent hopes elate,
  "Yet will I live will live, though *Emma's* dead
So long bow'd down beneath the storms of fate,
  Yet will I raise my woe-dejected head!
My little *Emma,* now my *all,*
  Will want a father's care,
Her looks, her wants, my rash resolves recal,
  And for'her sake the ills of life I'll bear:
And oft together we'll complain,
  Complain, the only bliss my soul can know.
From me my child shall learn the mournful strain,
  And prattle tales of woe ;
    And O! in that auspicious hour,
    When fate resigns her persecuting power,
With duteous zeal her hand shall close,
  No more to weep, my sorrow-streaming eyes,
When death gives misery repose,
  And opes a glorious passage to the skies."

Vain thought ! it must not be she too is dead
  The flattering scene is o'er,
My hopes for ever, ever fled
  And vengeance can no more,
Crush'd by misfortune blasted by disease
  And none none left to bear a friendly part!
To meditate my welfare, health, or ease,
  Or sooth the anguish of an aching heart!
Now all one gloomy scene, till welcome death,
  With lenient hand (O, falsely deem'd severe)
Shall kindly stop my grief-exhausted breath,
  And dry up eveiy tear:

Perhaps obsequious to my will,
   But, ah ! from my affections far remov'd!
The last sad office strangers may fulfil.
   As if I ne'er had been belov'd;
     As if, unconscious of poetic fire,
     I ne'er had touch'd the trembling lyre;
     As if my niggard hand ne'er dealt relief,
     Nor my heart melted at another's grief.

Yet while this weary life shall last,
   While yet my tongue can form th' impassion'd strain.

In piteous accents shall the muse complain,
   And dwell with fond delay on blessings past:
     For O how grateful to a wounded heart
     The tale of misery to impart!
     From others' eyes bid artless sorrows flow,
     And raise esteem upon the base of woe!
Even he,[1] the noblest of the tuneful throng,
   Shall deign my love-lorn tale to hear,
Shall catch the soft contagion of my song,
   And pay my pensive muse the tribute of a tear!

---

1   Lord Lyttelton

THE NIGHTINGALE AND GLOW-WORM

By William Cowper

A NIGHTINGALE, that all day long
Hath cheer'd the village with his song,
Nor yet at eve his note suspended,
Nor yet when eventide was ended,
Began to feel, as well he might,
The keen demands of appetite;
When, looking eagerly around,
He spied far off, upon the ground,
A something shining in the dark,
And knew the glow-worm by his spark;
So, stooping down from hawthorn top,
He thought to put him in his crop.
The worm, aware of his intent,
Harangu'd him thus, right eloquent—
 Did you admire my lamp, quoth he,
As much as I your minstrelsy,
You would abhor to do me wrong,
As much as I to spoil your song;
For 'twas the self-same pow'r divine
Taught you to sing, and me to shine;
That you with music, I with light,
Might beautify and cheer the night.
The songster heard his short oration,
And, warbling out his approbation,
Releas'd him, as my story tells,

And found a supper somewhere else.
   Hence jarring sectaries may learn
Their real int'rest to discern;
That brother should not war with brother,
And worry and devour each other;
But sing and shine by sweet consent,
Till life's poor transient night is spent,
Respecting in each other's case
The gifts of nature and of grace.
   Those Christians best deserve the name,
Who studiously make peace their aim;
Peace, both the duty and the prize
Of him that creeps and him that flies.

INVOCATION TO THE NIGHTINGALE

By Mary Hays

Wand'ring o'er the dewy meadow,
   Oft at ev'ning hour I go;
Fondly courting Philomela's
   Sympathetic plaints of woe.

Sometimes, hush'd in still attention,
   Leaning pensive o'er a stile,
Fancy bids her sound delusive
   Lull the yielding sense awhile.

Soft the visionary musick,
   Rising floats upon the gale:
Now it sinks in strains more languid,
   Dying o'er the distant vale.

Starting from the dream of fancy,
   Nought my list'ning ear invades,
Save the hum of falling waters,
   Save the rustling aspin-shade.

'Little songstress, soothe my sorrows,
   'Wrap my soul in softest airs'
'Such as erst, in Lydian measures,
   'Charm'd the Grecian hero's cares.

'But, if forcd by cruel rusticks
  'To lament thy ruin'd care;
'Breathe thy saddest strains of anguish,
  'Strains that melodize despair.

'Deeply vers'd in Sorrow's lessons,
  'Best my heart thy griefs can know;
'Pity dwells within the bosom
  'Soften'd by an equal woe.

'While thy melancholy plainings
  'All my hapless fate renew,
'Heart-felt sighs shall load the zephrs,
  'Tears increase the falling dew.

'Cease to shun me, lovely mourner;
  'Sweetly breathe the melting strain:
'Oft thou deign'st to charm the rustick,
  'Roving thoughtless o'er the plain.

'Yet, to him, thy softest trillings
  'Can no sympathy impart;
'Wouldst thou seek for kindred feelings,
  'See them trembling in my heart!'

Vain, alas! my Invocation,
  Vain the pleadings of the muse!
Wrapp'd in silent shades, the charmer
  Doth her tuneful lay refuse.

Clouds obscure deform the aether,
  Rising damps involve the plain;
Pensively I hasten homeward,
  To avoid the coming rain.

THE POET OF THE WOODS

ODE TO THE NIGHTINGALE

By Mary Darby Robinson

SWEET BIRD OF SORROW!—why complain
   In such soft melody of Song,
That ECHO, am'rous of thy Strain,
   The ling'ring cadence doth prolong?
Ah! tell me, tell me, why,
Thy dulcet Notes ascend the sky.
Or on the filmy vapours glide
Along the misty moutain's side?
And wherefore dost Thou love to dwell,
In the dark wood and moss-grown cell,
Beside the willow-margin'd stream—
Why dost Thou court wan Cynthia's beam?
Sweet Songstress–if thy wayward fate
Hath robb'd Thee of thy bosom's mate,
Oh! think not thy heart-piercing moan
   Evap'rates on the breezy air,
   Or that the plaintive Song of Care
Steals from THY Widow'd Breast alone.
Oft have I heard thy mournful Tale,
On the high Cliff, that o'er the Vale
Hangs its dark brow, whose awful shade
Spreads a deep gloom along the glade:
Led by its sound, I've wander'd far,
Till crimson evening's flaming Star
On Heav'n's vast dome refulgent hung,

And round ethereal vapours flung;
And oft I've sought the HYGEIAN MAID,
In rosy dimply smiles array'd,
Till forc'd with every HOPE to part,
Resistless Pain subdued my Heart.

Oh then, far o'er the restless deep
    Forlorn my poignant pangs I bore,
Alone in foreign realms to weep,
    Where ENVY's voice could taunt no more.
I hop'd, by mingling with the gay,
To snatch the veil of Grief away;
To break Affliction's pond'rous chain;
VAIN was the Hope—in vain I sought
The placid hour of careless thought,
Where Fashion wing'd her light career,
    And sportive Pleasure danc'd along,
    Oft have I shunn'd the blithsome throng,
To hide th'involuntary tear,
For e'en where rapt'rous transports glow,
From the full Heart the conscious tear will flow,
When to my downy couch remov'd,
    FANCY recall'd my wearied mind
    To scenes of FRIENDSHIP left behind,
Scenes still regretted, still belov'd!
Ah, then I felt the pangs of Grief,
    Grasp my warm Heart, and mock relief;
    My burning lids Sleep's balm defied,
And on my fev'rish lip imperfect murmurs died.

THE POET OF THE WOODS

Restless and sad—I sought once more
A calm retreat on BRITAIN's shore;
Deceitful HOPE, e'en there I found
   That soothing FRIENDSHIP's specious name
Was but a short-liv'd empty sound,
   And LOVE a false delusive flame.

Then come, Sweet BIRD, and with thy strain,
Steal from my breast the thorn of pain;
Blest solace of my lonely hours,
In craggy caves and silent bow'rs,
When HAPPY Mortals seek repose,
By Night's pale lamp we'll chaunt our woes,
And, as her chilling tears diffuse
O'er the white thorn their silv'ry dews,
I'll with the lucid boughts entwine
   A weeping Wreath, which round my Head
Shall by the waning Cresent shine,
   And light us to our leafy bed,—
Yet ah! nor leafy beds nor bow'rs
Fring'd with soft MAY's enamell'd flow'rs,
Nor pearly leaves, nor Cynthia's beams,
Nor smiling Pleasure's shad'wy dreams—
Sweet BIRD, not e'en THY melting Strains—
Can calm the Heart, where TYRANT SORROW REIGNS.

THE POET OF THE WOODS

SECOND ODE TO THE NIGHTINGALE

By Mary Darby Robinson

BLEST be thy song, sweet NIGHTINGALE,
Lorn minstrel of the lonely vale!
Where oft I've heard thy dulcet strain
In mournful melody complain;
When in the POPLAR'S trembling shade,
At Evening's purple hour I've stray'd,
While many a silken folded flow'r
Wept on its couch of Gossamer,
And many a time in pensive mood
Upon the upland mead I've stood,
To mark grey twilight's shadows glide
Along the green hill's velvet side;
To watch the perfum'd hand of morn
Hang pearls upon the silver thorn,
Till rosy day with lustrous eye
In saffron mantle deck'd the sky,
And bound the mountain's brow with fire,
And ting'd with gold the village spire:
While o'er the frosted vale below
The amber tints began to glow:
And oft I seek the daisied plain
To greet the rustic nymph and swain,
When cowslips gay their bells unfold,
And flaunt their leaves of glitt'ring gold,
While from the blushes of the rose

THE POET OF THE WOODS

A tide of musky essence flows,
And o'er the odour-breathing flow'rs
The woodlands shed their diamond show'rs,
When from the scented hawthorn bud
The BLACKBIRD sips the lucid flood,
While oft the twitt'ring THRUSH essays
To emulate the LINNET'S lays;
While the poiz'd LARK her carol sings
And BUTTERFLIES expand their wings,
And BEES begin their sultry toils
And load their limbs with luscious spoils,
I stroll along the pathless vale,
And smile, and bless thy soothing tale.

But ah! when hoary winter chills
The plumy race—and wraps the hills
In snowy vest, I tell my pains
Beside the brook in icy chains
Bound its weedy banks between,
While sad I watch night's pensive queen,
Just emblem of MY weary woes:
For ah ! where'er the virgin goes,
Each flow'ret greets her with a tear
To sympathetic sorrow dear;
And when in black obtrusive clouds
The chilly MOON her pale cheek shrouds,
I mark the twinkling starry train
Exulting glitter in her wane,
And proudly gleam their borrow'd light
To gem the sombre dome of night.
Then o'er the meadows cold and bleak,
The glow-worm's glimm'ring lamp I seek.
Or climb the craggy cliff to gaze
On some bright planet's azure blaze,
And o'er the dizzy height inclin'd

THE POET OF THE WOODS

I listen to the passing wind,
That loves my mournful song to seize,
And bears it to the mountain breeze.
Or where the sparry caves among
Dull ECHO sits with aëry tongue,
Or gliding on the ZEPHYR'S wings
From hill to hill her cadence flings,
O, then my melancholy tale
Dies on the bosom of the gale,
While awful stillness reigning round
   Blanches my cheek with chilling fear;
Till from the bushy dell profound,
   The woodman's song salutes mine ear.
When dark NOVEMBER'S boist'rous breath
Sweeps the blue hill and desart heath,
When naked trees their white tops wave
O'er many a famish'd REDBREAST'S grave,
When many a clay-built cot lays low
Beneath the growing hills of snow,
Soon as the SHEPHERD's silv'ry head
Peeps from his tottering straw-roof'd shed,
To hail the glimm'ring glimpse of day—
   With feeble steps he ventures forth
   Chill'd by the bleak breath of the North,
And to the forest bends his way,
To gather from the frozen ground
Each branch the night-blast scatter'd round—
If in some bush o'erspread with snow
He hears thy moaning wail of woe,
A flush of warmth his cheek o'erspreads,
With anxious timid care he treads,
And when his cautious hands infold
Thy little breast benumb'd with cold,
"Come, plaintive fugitive," he cries,
While PITY dims his aged eyes,

THE POET OF THE WOODS

"Come to my glowing heart, and share
"My narrow cell, my humble fare,
"Tune thy sweet carol–plume thy wing,
"And quaff with me the limpid spring,
"And peck the crumbs my meals supply,
"And round my rushy pillow fly."

  O, MINSTREL SWEET, whose jocund lay
Can make e'en POVERTY look gay,
Who can the poorest swain inspire
And while he fans his scanty fire,
When o'er the plain rough Winter pours
Nocturnal blasts, and whelming show'rs,
Canst thro' his little mansion fling
The rapt'rous melodies of spring.
To THEE with eager gaze I turn,
  Blest solace of the aching breast;
Each gaudy, glitt'ring scene I spurn,
  And sigh for solitude and rest,
For art thou not, blest warbler, say,
  My mind's best balm, my bosom's friend?
Didst thou not trill thy softest lay,
  And with thy woes my sorrows blend?
YES, darling Songstress! when of late
  I sought thy leafy-fringed bow'r,
The victim of relentless fate,
  Fading in life's dark ling'ring hour,
Thou heard'st my plaint, and pour'd thy strain
  Thro' the sad mansion of my breast,
  And softly, sweetly lull'd to rest
The throbbing anguish of my brain.

THE POET OF THE WOODS

AH! while I tread this vale of woe,
Still may thy downy measures flow,
To wing my solitary hours
With kind, obliterating pow'rs;
And tho' my pensive, patient heart
No wild, extatic bliss shall prove,
Tho' life no raptures shall impart,
No boundless joy, or, madd'ning love,
Sweet NIGHTINGALE, thy lenient strain
Shall mock Despair, AND BLUNT THE SHAFT OF PAIN.

THE POET OF THE WOODS

TO THE NIGHTINGALE

By Ann Radcliffe

Child of the melancholy song!
O yet that tender strain prolong!

    Her lengthen'd shade when Ev'ning flings,
        From mountain-cliffs, and forests green,
    And sailing slow on silent wings,
        Along the glimm'ring West is seen;
    I love o'er pathless hills to stray,
        Or trace the winding vale remote,
    And pause, sweet Bird! to hear thy lay,
        While moon-beams on the thin clouds float;
    'Till o'er the Mountain's dewy head
    Pale Midnight steals to wake the dead.

    Far through the Heav'ns' aetherial blue,
        Wafted on Spring's light airs you come,
    With blooms, and flow'rs, and genial dew,
        From climes where Summer joys to roam,
        O! welcome to your long lost home!
    'Child of the melancholy song!'
        Who lov'st the lonely woodland-glade
    To mourn, unseen, the boughs among,
        When Twilight spreads her pensive shade,
    Again thy dulcet voice I hail!
            O! pour again the liquid note

That dies upon the ev'ning gale!
  For Fancy loves the kindred tone;
  Her griefs the plaintive accents own.
    She loves to hear thy music float
At solemn midnight's stillest hour,
  And think on friends for ever lost,
  On joys by disappointment crost,
And weep anew Love's charmful pow'r!

Then Memory wakes the magic smile,
  Th' impassion'd voice, the melting eye,
That won't the trusting heart beguile,
  And wakes again the hopeless sigh!
Her skill the glowing tints revive
  Of scenes that Time had bade decay:
She bids the soften'd Passions live—
  The Passions urge again their sway.
Yet o'er the long-regretted scene,
  Thy song the grace of sorrow throws;
A melancholy charm serene,
  More rare than all that mirth bestows.
Then hail, sweet Bird! and hail thy pensive tear!
To Taste, to Fancy, and to Virtue dear!"

TO THE NIGHTINGALE, WHICH THE AUTHOR HEARD SING ON NEW YEAR'S DAY

By William Cowper

Whence it is, that amazed I hear
From yonder withered spray,
This foremost morn of all the year,
The melody of May?

And why, since thousands would be proud
Of such a favour shown,
Am I selected from the crowd
To witness it alone?

Sing'st thou, sweet Philomel, to me,
For that I also long
Have practised in the groves like thee,
Though not like thee in song?

Or sing'st thou rather under force
Of some divine command,
Commissioned to presage a course
Of happier days at hand?

Thrice welcome then! for many a long
And joyless year have I,
As thou to-day, put forth my song
Beneath a wintry sky.

THE POET OF THE WOODS

But Thee no wintry skies can harm,
Who only need'st to sing,
To make even January charm,
And every season Spring.

TO A NIGHTINGALE

By Charlotte Smith

Poor melancholy bird, that all night long
   Tell'st to the moon thy tale of tender woe;
   From what sad cause can such sweet sorrow flow,
And whence this mournful melody of song?

Thy poet's musing fancy would translate
   What mean the sounds that swell thy little breast,
   When still at dewy eve thou leav'st thy nest,
Thus to the listening night to sing thy fate.

Pale Sorrow's victims wert thou once among,
   Though now released in woodlands wild to rove;
   Say, hast thou felt from friends some cruel wrong,
Or diedst thou martyr of disastrous love?
Ah, songstress sad, that such my lot might be;
To sigh and sing at liberty—like thee!

ON THE DEPARTURE OF THE NIGHTINGALE

By Charlotte Smith

SWEET poet of the woods — a long adieu!
   Farewell, soft minstrel of the early year!
Ah! 'twill be long ere thou shalt sing anew,
   And pour thy music on the 'night's dull ear.'
Whether on Spring thy wandering flights await,
   Or whether silent in our groves you dwell,
The pensive muse shall own thee for her mate,
   And still protect the song she loves so well.
With cautious step the lovelorn youth shall glide
   1Thro' the lone brake that shades thy mossy nest;
And shepherd girls, from eyes profane shall hide
   The gentle bird, who sings of pity best:
For still thy voice shall soft affections move,
And still be dear to sorrow, and to love!

THE RETURN OF THE NIGHTINGALE

By Charlotte Smith

Writen in May

BORNE on the warm wing of the western gale,
   How tremulously low is heard to float,
Thro' the green budding thorns that fringe the vale,
   The early Nightingale's prelusive note.

'Tis Hope's instinctive pow'r that, thro' the grove,
   Tells how benignant Heav'n revives the earth;
'Tis the soft voice of young and timid love
   That calls these melting sounds of sweetness forth.

With transport, once, sweet bird! I hail'd thy lay,
   And bade thee welome to our shades again,
To charm the wand'ring poet's pensive way,
   And soothe the solitary lover's pain;
But now! — such evils in my lot combine,
As shut my languid sense, to Hope's dear voice and thine.

TO THE NIGHTINGALE

By Robert Southey

Sad songstress of the night, no more I hear
Thy soften'd warblings meet my pensive ear,
    As by thy wonted haunts again I rove;
Why art thou silent? wherefore sleeps thy lay?
For faintly fades the sinking orb of day,
    And yet thy music charms no more the grove.
The shrill bat flutters by; from yon dark tower
The shrieking owlet hails the shadowy hour;
    Hoarse hums the beetle as he drones along,
The hour of love is flown! thy full-fledg'd brood
No longer need thy care to cull their food,
    And nothing now remains to prompt the song:
But drear and sullen seems the silent grove,
No more responsive to the lay of love.

THE NIGHTINGALE;
A CONVERSATIONAL POEM

By Samuel Taylor Coleridge

Written in April

No cloud, no relique of the sunken day
Distinguishes the West, no long thin slip
Of sullen Light, no obscure trembling hues.
Come, we will rest on this old mossy Bridge!
You see the glimmer of the stream beneath,
But hear no murmuring: it flows silently
O'er its soft bed of verdure. All is still,
A balmy night! and tho' the stars be dim,
Yet let us think upon the vernal showers
That gladden the green earth, and we shall find
A pleasure in the dimness of the stars.
And hark! the Nightingale begins its song,
"Most musical, most melancholy"[2] Bird!

---

2   "Most musical, most melancholy." This passage in Milton possesses an excellence far superior to that of mere description: it is spoken in the character of the melancholy Man, and has therefore a dramatic propriety. The Author makes this remark, to rescue himself from the charge of having alluded with levity to a line in Milton: a charge than which none could be more painful to him, except perhaps that of having ridiculed his Bible.

THE POET OF THE WOODS

A melancholy Bird? O idle thought!
In nature there is nothing melancholy.
—But some night-wandering Man, whose heart was pierc'd
With the remembrance of a grievous wrong,
Or slow distemper or neglected love,
(And so, poor Wretch! fill'd all things with himself
And made all gentle sounds tell back the tale
Of his own sorrows) he and such as he
First nam'd these notes a melancholy strain;
And many a poet echoes the conceit,
Poet, who hath been building up the rhyme
When he had better far have stretch'd his limbs
Beside a brook in mossy forest-dell
By sun or moonlight, to the influxes
Of shapes and sounds and shifting elements
Surrendering his whole spirit, of his song
And of his fame forgetful! so his fame
Should share in nature's immortality,
A venerable thing! and so his song
Should make all nature lovelier, and itself
Be lov'd, like nature!—But 'twill not be so;
And youths and maidens most poetical
"Who lose the deep'ning twilights of the spring
In ball-rooms and hot theatres, they still
Full of meek sympathy must heave their sighs
O'er Philomela's pity-pleading strains.
My Friend, and my Friend's Sister! we have learnt
A different lore: we may not thus profane
Nature's sweet voices always full of love
And joyance! Tis the merry Nightingale
That crowds, and hurries, and precipitates
With fast thick warble his delicious notes,
As he were fearful, that an April night
Would be too short for him to utter forth

THE POET OF THE WOODS

His love-chant, and disburthen his full soul
Of all its music! And I know a grove
Of large extent, hard by a castle huge
Which the great lord inhabits not: and so
This grove is wild with tangling underwood,
And the trim walks are broken up, and grass,
Thin grass and king-cups grow within the paths.
But never elsewhere in one place I knew
So many Nightingales: and far and near
In wood and thicket over the wide grove
They answer and provoke each other's songs—
With skirmish and capricious passagings,
And murmurs musical and swift jug jug
And one low piping sound more sweet than all—
Stirring the air with such an harmony,
That should you close your eyes, you might almost
Forget it was not day! On moonlight bushes,
Whose dewy leafits are but half disclos'd,
You may perchance behold them on the twigs,
Their bright, bright eyes, their eyes both bright and full,
Glistning, while many a glow-worm in the shade
Lights up her love-torch.

   A most gentle maid
Who dwelleth in her hospitable home
Hard by the Castle, and at latest eve,
(Even like a Lady vow'd and dedicate
To something more than nature in the grove)
Glides thro' the pathways; she knows all their notes,
That gentle Maid! and oft, a moment's space,
What time the moon was lost behind a cloud,
Hath heard a pause of silence: till the Moon
Emerging, hath awaken'd earth and sky
"With one sensation, and those wakeful Birds
Have all burst forth in choral minstrelsy,

THE POET OF THE WOODS

As if one quick and sudden Gale had swept
An hundred airy harps! And she hath watch'd
Many a Nightingale perch giddily
On blosmy twig still swinging from the breeze,
And to that motion tune his wanton song,
Like tipsy Joy that reels with tossing head.

Farewell, O Warbler! till to-morrow eve,
And you, my friends! farewell, a short farewell!
We have been loitering long and pleasantly,
And now for our dear homes.—That strain again!
Full fain it would delay me!—My dear Babe,
Who, capable of no articulate sound,
Mars all things with his imitative lisp,
How he would place his hand beside his ear.
His little hand, the small forefinger up,
And bid us listen! And I deem it wise
To make him Nature's playmate. He knows well
The evening star: and once when he awoke
In most distressful mood (some inward pain
Had made up that strange thing, an infant's dream)
I hurried with him to our orchard plot,
And he beholds the moon, and hush'd at once
Suspends his sobs, and laughs most silently,
While his fair eyes that swam with undropt tears
Did glitter in the yellow moon-beam! Well—
It is a father's tale. But if that Heaven
Should give me life, his childhood shall grow up
Familiar with these songs, that with the night
He may associate Joy! Once more farewell,
Sweet Nightingale! once more, my friends! farewell.

THE FAIRY, THE ROSE, AND THE NIGHTINGALE; A FABLE

By Royall Tyler

A ROSE while yet 'twas early morn,
Was glowing on her dewy thorn.
The smallest of the elfin kind
That thro' the garden flowers wind,
Beheld where, like another day,
She op'd in morning on the spray,
Amid her orient leaflets flew,
And sipt his fill of scented dew;
"Sweet blossom," then he softly cry'd,
With voice that mid the petals died,
"Sweet blossom, for this draught divine,
Some splendid present shall be thine,
Thou art so fair all flowers before,
That 'twould be vain to deck thee more,
But when the shades of night appear,
To blend the ugly and the fair,
That thy bright charms may still be seen,
And thou still reign of flowers the queen,
My lamp I'll bring, the glow-worm bright,
And hang amid thy leaves its light."
The rose receiv'd, with modest bend,
The promise of her fairy friend,
Who brought at twilight's tranquil hour
The lanthorn of her little bower,
That threw its threadlike beams around,

And shed a radiance on the ground;
A Nightingale, who warbled nigh,
'Midst darksome boughs, with greedy eye
Beheld the glitt'ring prize that hung
With diamond light her leaves among,
And straight in lays that lull'd the grove,
Caroll'd a tender tale of love.
Soft flower, her breast withstands not long
The varying music of his song;
But soon what pangs assail'd that breast!
For scarce the nuptial kiss he prest,
But tore from its supporting spray,
The Fairy's gift, and hopt away.
O Rose, it was thy lot to prove
The lowest Vice may feign like Love,
Nor is it such sorrow thine alone;
Full many a maid thy fate has known,
Whom fortune (by the hand of heaven,
With unveiled eyes a moment given,
Her blind-groped favourites to behold)
Has lent the gorgeous light of gold,
That virtue's charms with beauty join'd
Might wide be seen and win mankind;
But ah! that light's resplendent dawn,
Interest the heartless slave has drawn,
Who sings Love's soul-enthralling lay,
So to revel in the golden ray.

O NIGHTINGALE! THOU SURELY ART

By William Wordsworth

O NIGHTINGALE! thou surely art
A Creature of ebullient heart:—
These notes of thine—they pierce and pierce;
Tumultuous harmony and fierce!
Thou sing'st as if the God of wine
Had helped thee to a Valentine;
A song in mockery and despite
Of shades, and dews, and silent Night;
And steady bliss, and all the loves
Now sleeping in these peaceful Groves.

I heard a Stock-dove sing or say
His homely tale, this very day.
His voice was buried among trees,
Yet to be come at by the breeze:
He did not cease; but coo'd—and coo'd;
And somewhat pensively he woo'd:
He sang of love with quiet blending,
Slow to begin, and never ending;
Of serious faith and inward glee;
That was the Song—the Song for me!

ODE TO A NIGHTINGALE

By John Keats

I

My heart aches, and a drowsy numbness pains
   My sense, as though of hemlock I had drunk,
Or emptied some dull opiate to the drains
   One minute past, and Lethe-wards had sunk:
'Tis not through envy of thy happy lot,
   But being too happy in thine happiness,—
      That thou, light-winged Dryad of the trees
         In some melodious plot
Of beechen green, and shadows numberless,
   Singest of summer in full-throated ease.

II

O, for a draught of vintage! that hath been
  Cool'd a long age in the deep-delved earth,
Tasting of Flora and the country green,
  Dance, and Provençal song, and sunburnt mirth!
O for a beaker full of the warm South,
  Full of the true, the blushful Hippocrene,
    With beaded bubbles winking at the brim,
      And purple-stained mouth;
  That I might drink, and leave the world unseen,
    And with thee fade away into the forest dim:

III

Fade far away, dissolve, and quite forget
  What thou among the leaves hast never known,
The weariness, the fever, and the fret
  Here, where men sit and hear each other groan;
Where palsy shakes a few, sad, last gray hairs,
  Where youth grows pale, and spectre-thin, and dies;
    Where but to think is to be full of sorrow
      And leaden-eyed despairs,
  Where Beauty cannot keep her lustrous eyes,
    Or new Love pine at them beyond to-morrow.

THE POET OF THE WOODS

IV

Away! away! for I will fly to thee,
  Not charioted by Bacchus and his pards,
But on the viewless wings of Poesy,
  Though the dull brain perplexes and retards:
Already with thee! tender is the night,
  And haply the Queen-Moon is on her throne,
    Cluster'd around by all her starry Fays;
      But here there is no light,
Save what from heaven is with the breezes blown
  Through verdurous glooms and winding mossy ways.

V

I cannot see what flowers are at my feet,
  Nor what soft incense hangs upon the boughs,
But, in embalmed darkness, guess each sweet
  Wherewith the seasonable month endows
The grass, the thicket, and the fruit-tree wild;
  White hawthorn, and the pastoral eglantine;
    Fast fading violets cover'd up in leaves;
      And mid-May's eldest child,
The coming musk-rose, full of dewy wine,
  The murmurous haunt of flies on summer eves.

VI

Darkling I listen; and, for many a time
  I have been half in love with easeful Death,
Call'd him soft names in many a mused rhyme,
  To take into the air my quiet breath;
Now more than ever seems it rich to die,
  To cease upon the midnight with no pain,
      While thou art pouring forth thy soul abroad
          In such an ecstasy!
Still wouldst thou sing, and I have ears in vain—
  To thy high requiem become a sod.

VII

Thou wast not born for death, immortal Bird!
  No hungry generations tread thee down;
The voice I hear this passing night was heard
  In ancient days by emperor and clown:
Perhaps the self-same song that found a path
  Through the sad heart of Ruth, when, sick for home,
    She stood in tears amid the alien corn;
        The same that oft-times hath
Charm'd magic casements, opening on the foam
  Of perilous seas, in faery lands forlorn.

VIII

Forlorn! the very word is like a bell
To toll me back from thee to my sole self!
Adieu! the fancy cannot cheat so well
As she is fam'd to do, deceiving elf.
Adieu! adieu! thy plaintive anthem fades
Past the near meadows, over the still stream,
Up the hill-side; and now 'tis buried deep
In the next valley-glades:
Was it a vision, or a waking dream?
Fled is that music:—Do I wake or sleep?

THE NIGHTINGALE

By Horace Smith

LONE warbler! thy love-melting heart supplies
   The liquid music-fall, that from thy bill
Gushes in such ecstatic rhapsodies,
   Drowning night's ear. Yet thine is but the skill
Of loftier love, that hung up in the skies
   Those everlasting lamps, man's guide, until
Morning return, and bade fresh flowers arise,
   Blooming by night, new fragrance to distil.

Why are these blessings lavished from above
   On man, when his unconscious sense and sight
Are closed in sleep; but that the few who rove,
   From want or woe, or travels urge by night,
   May still have perfumes, music, flowers, and light;
So kind and watchful is celestial love!

THE WOODMAN
AND THE NIGHTINGALE

By Percy Bysshe Shelley

A woodman whose rough heart was out of tune
(I think such hearts yet never came to good)
Hated to hear, under the stars or moon,

One nightingale in an interfluous wood
Satiate the hungry dark with melody;—
And as a vale is watered by a flood,

Or as the moonlight fills the open sky
Struggling with darkness—as a tuberose
Peoples some Indian dell with scents which lie

Like clouds above the flower from which they rose,
The singing of that happy nightingale
In this sweet forest, from the golden close

Of evening till the star of dawn may fail,
Was interfused upon the silentness;
The folded roses and the violets pale

Heard her within their slumbers, the abyss
Of heaven with all its planets; the dull ear
Of the night-cradled earth; the loneliness

Of the circumfluous waters,—every sphere
And every flower and beam and cloud and wave,
And every wind of the mute atmosphere,

And every beast stretched in its rugged cave,
And every bird lulled on its mossy bough,
And every silver moth fresh from the grave

Which is its cradle—ever from below
Aspiring like one who loves too fair, too far,
To be consumed within the purest glow

Of one serene and unapproached star,
As if it were a lamp of earthly light,
Unconscious, as some human lovers are,

Itself how low, how high beyond all height
The heaven where it would perish!—and every form
That worshipped in the temple of the night

Was awed into delight, and by the charm
Girt as with an interminable zone,
Whilst that sweet bird, whose music was a storm

Of sound, shook forth the dull oblivion
Out of their dreams; harmony became love
In every soul but one.

* * * * *

And so this man returned with axe and saw
At evening close from killing the tall treen,
The soul of whom by Nature's gentle law

THE POET OF THE WOODS

Was each a wood-nymph, and kept ever green
The pavement and the roof of the wild copse,
Chequering the sunlight of the blue serene

With jagged leaves,—and from the forest tops
Singing the winds to sleep—or weeping oft
Fast showers of aereal water-drops

Into their mother's bosom, sweet and soft,
Nature's pure tears which have no bitterness;—
Around the cradles of the birds aloft

They spread themselves into the loveliness
Of fan-like leaves, and over pallid flowers
Hang like moist clouds:—or, where high branches kiss,

Make a green space among the silent bowers,
Like a vast fane in a metropolis,
Surrounded by the columns and the towers

All overwrought with branch-like traceries
In which there is religion—and the mute
Persuasion of unkindled melodies,

Odours and gleams and murmurs, which the lute
Of the blind pilot-spirit of the blast
Stirs as it sails, now grave and now acute,

Wakening the leaves and waves, ere it has passed
To such brief unison as on the brain
One tone, which never can recur, has cast,
One accent never to return again.

* * * * *

THE POET OF THE WOODS

The world is full of Woodmen who expel
Love's gentle Dryads from the haunts of life,
And vex the nightingales in every dell.

STRADA'S NIGHTINGALE

By William Cowper

THE shepherd touched his reed; sweet Philomel
    Essayed, and oft essayed to catch the strain,
And treasuring, as on her ear they fell,
    The numbers, echoed note for note again.

The peevish youth, who ne'er had found before
    A rival of his skill, indignant heard,
And soon (for various was his tuneful store)
    In loftier tones defied the simple bird.

She dared the task, and rising, as he rose,
    With all the force that passion gives inspired,
Returned the sounds awhile, but in the close,
    Exhausted fell, and at his feet expired.

Thus strength, not skill, prevailed. O fatal strife,
    By thee, poor songstress, playfully begun!
And oh, sad victory, which cost thy life,
    And he may wish that he had never won.

TO THE NIGHTINGALE

By Charles Tennyson Turner

O! honey-throated mourner of the grove!
That in the glooming woodland art so proud
Of answering thy sweet mates in soft or loud,
Thou dost not own a note we do not love!
The moon is o'er thee — laying out the lawn
In mighty shadows — and the twilight skies,
Imbued with their unutterable dyes,
A thousand hues from Summer sources drawn;
"While wandering for the dreams such seasons give
With lonely steps thro ; this transcendant scene,
The Poet weeps for joys that fled yestreen
And staid not here to bless this purple eve,
Too lately fled, and brought him here to grieve
In passionate regret for what hath been.

SONG

By Hartley Coleridge

'Tis sweet to hear the merry lark,
    That bids a blithe good-morrow;
But sweeter to hark, in the twinkling dark,
    To the soothing song of sorrow.
Oh nightingale! What doth she ail?
    And is she sad or jolly?
For ne'er on earth was sound of mirth
    So like to melancholy.

The merry lark, he soars on high,
    No worldly thought o'ertakes him;
He sings aloud to the clear blue sky,
    And the daylight that awakes him.
As sweet a lay, as loud, as gay,
    The nightingale is trilling;
With feeling bliss, no less than his,
    Her little heart is thrilling.

Yet ever and anon, a sigh
    Peers through her lavish mirth;
For the lark's bold song is of the sky,
    And hers is of the earth.
By night and day, she tunes her lay,
    To drive away all sorrow;
For bliss, alas! to-night must pass,
    And woe may come to-morrow.

THE NIGHTINGALE'S NEST

By John Clare

Up this green woodland—ride let's softly rove,
And list the nightingale—she dwells just here.
Hush! let the wood-gate softly clap, for fear
The noise might drive her from her home of love;
For here I've heard her many a merry year—
At morn, at eve, nay, all the live-long day,
As though she lived on song. This very spot,
Just where that old-man's-beard all wildly trails
Rude arbours o'er the road, and stops the way—
And where that child its blue-bell flowers hath got,
Laughing and creeping through the mossy rails—
There have I hunted like a very boy,
Creeping on hands and knees through matted thorn
To find her nest, and see her feed her young.
And vainly did I many hours employ:
All seemed as hidden as a thought unborn.
And where those crimping fern-leaves ramp among
The hazel's under boughs, I've nestled down,
And watched her while she sung; and her renown
Hath made me marvel that so famed a bird
Should have no better dress than russet brown.
Her wings would tremble in her ecstasy,
And feathers stand on end, as 'twere with joy,
And mouth wide open to release her heart
Of its out-sobbing songs. The happiest part

THE POET OF THE WOODS

Of summer's fame she shared, for so to me
Did happy fancies shapen her employ;
But if I touched a bush, or scarcely stirred,
All in a moment stopt. I watched in vain:
The timid bird had left the hazel bush,
And at a distance hid to sing again.
Lost in a wilderness of listening leaves,
Rich Ecstasy would pour its luscious strain,
Till envy spurred the emulating thrush
To start less wild and scarce inferior songs;
For while of half the year Care him bereaves,
To damp the ardour of his speckled breast;
The nightingale to summer's life belongs,
And naked trees, and winter's nipping wrongs,
Are strangers to her music and her rest.
Her joys are evergreen, her world is wide—
Hark! there she is as usual—let's be hush—
For in this black-thorn clump, if rightly guest,
Her curious house is hidden. Part aside
These hazel branches in a gentle way,
And stoop right cautious 'neath the rustling boughs,
For we will have another search to day,
And hunt this fern-strewn thorn-clump round and round;
And where this reeded wood-grass idly bows,
We'll wade right through, it is a likely nook:
In such like spots, and often on the ground,
They'll build, where rude boys never think to look—
Aye, as I live! her secret nest is here,
Upon this white-thorn stump! I've searched about
For hours in vain. There! put that bramble by—
Nay, trample on its branches and get near.
How subtle is the bird! she started out,
And raised a plaintive note of danger nigh,
Ere we were past the brambles; and now, near
Her nest, she sudden stops—as choking fear,

That might betray her home. So even now
We'll leave it as we found it: safety's guard
Of pathless solitudes shall keep it still.
See there! she's sitting on the old oak bough,
Mute in her fears; our presence doth retard
Her joys, and doubt turns every rapture chill.
Sing on, sweet bird! may no worse hap befall
Thy visions, than the fear that now deceives.
We will not plunder music of its dower,
Nor turn this spot of happiness to thrall;
For melody seems hid in every flower,
That blossoms near thy home. These harebells all
Seem bowing with the beautiful in song;
And gaping cuckoo-flower, with spotted leaves,
Seems blushing of the singing it has heard.
How curious is the nest; no other bird
Uses such loose materials, or weaves
Its dwelling in such spots: dead oaken leaves
Are placed without, and velvet moss within,
And little scraps of grass, and, scant and spare,
What scarcely seem materials, down and hair;
For from men's haunts she nothing seems to win.
Yet Nature is the builder, and contrives
Homes for her children's comfort, even here;
Where Solitude's disciples spend their lives
Unseen, save when a wanderer passes near
That loves such pleasant places. Deep adown,
The nest is made a hermit's mossy cell.
Snug lie her curious eggs in number five,
Of deadened green, or rather olive brown;
And the old prickly thorn-bush guards them well.
So here we'll leave them, still unknown to wrong,
As the old woodland's legacy of song.

THE NIGHTINGALE; CHILD'S EVENING HYMN

By Felicia Dorothea Hemans

WHEN twilight's grey and pensive hour
Brings the low breeze, and shuts the flower,
And bids the solitary star
Shine in pale beauty from afar;

When gathering shades the landscape veil,
And peasants seek their village-dale,
And mists from river-wave arise,
And dew in every blossom lies;

When evening's primrose opes, to shed
Soft fragrance round her grassy bed;
When glow-worms in the wood-walk light!
Their lamp, to cheer the traveller's sight;

At that calm hour, so still, so pale,
Awakes the lonely Nightingale;
And from a hermitage of shade
Fills with her voice the forest-glade:

And sweeter far that melting voice,
Than all which through the day rejoice;
And still shall bard and wanderer love
The twilight music of the grove.

THE POET OF THE WOODS

Father in heaven! oh! thus when day
With all its cares hath passed away,
And silent hours waft peace on earth,
And hush the louder strains of mirth;

Thus may sweet songs of praise and prayer
To Thee my spirit's offering bear;
Yon star, my signal, set on high,
For vesper-hymns of piety.

So man Thy mercy and Thy power
Protect me through the midnight hour;
And balmy sleep and visions blest
Smile on Thy servant's bed of rest.

TO THE NIGHTINGALE

By John Clare

I love to hear the Nightingale—
  She comes where Summer dwells—
Among the brakes and orchis flowers,
  And foxglove's freckled bells.

Where mugwort grows like mignonette,
  And molehills swarm with ling;
She hides among the greener May,
  And sings her love to Spring.

I hear her in the Forest Beach,
  When beautiful and new;
Where cow-boys hunt the glossy leaf,
  Where falls the honey-dew.

Where brambles keep the waters cool
  For half the Summer long;
The maiden sets her pitcher down,
  And stops to hear the song.

The redcap is a painted bird,
  And sings about the town;
The Nightingale sings all the eve,
  In sober suit of brown.

THE POET OF THE WOODS

I knew the sparrow could not sing;
    And heard the stranger long:
I could not think so plain a bird
    Could sing so fine a song.

I found her nest of oaken leaves,
    And eggs of paler brown,
Where none would ever look for nests,
    Or pull the sedges down.

I found them on a whitethorn root,
    And in the woodland hedge,
All in a low and stumpy bush,
    Half hid among the sedge.

I love the Poet of the Woods,
    And love to hear her sing,—
That, with the cuckoo, brings the love
    And music of the Spring.

Man goes by art to foreign lands,
    With shipwreck and decay;
Birds go with Nature for their guide,
    And GOD directs their way—

GOD of a thousand worlds on high!—
    Proud men may lord and dare;
POWER tells them that the meaner things
    Are worthy of HIS care.

THE POET OF THE WOODS

THE NIGHTINGALE

By George Lunt

OFT have I read in many a foreign tale,
    Oh nightingale!
From thy love-laden heart how song's full soul
    Warbled would roll;
While, through the livelong night, from thy clear throat,
    The ravishing note,
With such entrancing melody would gush,
    That winds grew hush,
As every funeral fall and conquering rise
    Challenged the skies.

Thus often, where the fragrant summer roves
    Thessalian groves,
And wind-swept isles of beauty nightly sigh
    Sweet elegy;
And lovers' vows grew rapturous, as they heard,
    Listening the bird;
So could the solemn song enchant the sense
    To joy intense;
And Grief's sad heart, by that Æolian strain,
    Rapt of its pain,
Forgot the memory of its midnight tears
    And wasting years.

There, under bowers and wreathed canopies
                Of moonlit trees,
And starry constellations gleaming through
                The twilight dew,
The poet's heart in that delicious stream
                Bathed every dream,
And thence some hue of heaven his fancy stole,
                With music's soul;
And the deep measure, loaded with such freight,
                Floated elate;
Far o'er the worldly way and common haunt
                Swelled the clear chant,
Like the first bird that, ere the day is born,
                Mounts to the morn,
Leaves night below, and catches, as she springs,
                Heaven on her wings.

Oh for a vintage draught, full-fraught like this,
                To meet my kiss,
Filled to the blushing brim with dreams of old
                And bubbling gold!
Some breath of voice divine, or chorded shell,
                Of golden spell,
That to the longing soul responds and clings,
                And gives it wings;
Or such deep minstrelsies, oh nightingale,
                As thy lorn wail;
That fill the minstrel-heart, till raptures make
                The heart-strings break,
Breathing life out in the long melody
                Of one sweet sigh.

TO THE NIGHTINGALE

By Frances Anne Kemble

How passing sad! Listen, it sings again!
    Art thou a spirit that, amongst the boughs,
The livelong night dost chant that wondrous strain,
    Making wan Dian stoop her silver brows
Out of the clouds to hear thee? who shall say,
Thou lone one! that thy melody is gay,
Let him come listen now to that one note,
    That thou art pouring o'er and o'er again
Through the sweet echoes of thy mellow throat,
    With such a sobbing sound of deep, deep pain.
I prithee cease thy song! for from my heart
Thou hast made memory's bitter waters start,
    And filled my weary eyes with the soul's rain.

THE POET OF THE WOODS

EASTERN SUNSET

By Frances Anne Kemble

'Tis only the nightingale's warbled strain,
   That floats through the evening sky:
With his note of love, he replies again,
   To the muezzin's holy cry;
As it sweetly sounds on the rosy air,
"Allah, il allah! come to prayer!"
Warm o'er the waters the red sun is glowing,
'Tis the last parting glance of his splendour and might,
While each rippling wave on the bright shore is throwing
Its white crest, that breaks into showers of light.
Each distant mosque and minaret
Is shining in the setting sun,
Whose farewell look is brighter yet,
Than that with which his course begun.
On the dark blue mountains his smile is bright,
It glows on the orange grove's waving height,
And breaks through its shade in long lines of light.
No sound on the earth, and no sound in the sky,
Save murmuring fountains that sparkle nigh,
And the rustling flight of the evening breeze,
Who steals from his nest in the cypress trees,
And a thousand dewy odours fling,
As he shakes their white buds from his gossamer wing,
And flutters away through the spicy air,
At sound of a footstep drawing near.

TO A NIGHTINGALE

By George Meredith

O nightingale! how hast thou learnt
    The note of the nested dove?
While under thy bower the fern hangs burnt
    And no cloud hovers above!
Rich July has many a sky
With splendour dim, that thou mightst hymn,
And make rejoice with thy wondrous voice,
    And the thrill of thy wild pervading tone!
But instead of to woo, thou hast learnt to coo:
Thy song is mute at the mellowing fruit,
And the dirge of the flowers is sung by the hours
    In silence and twilight alone.

O nightingale! 'tis this, 'tis this
    That makes thee mock the dove!
That thou hast past thy marriage bliss,
    To know a parent's love.
The waves of fern may fade and burn,
The grasses may fall, the flowers and all,
And the pine-smells o'er the oak dells
    Float on their drowsy and odorous wings,
But thou wilt do nothing but coo,
Brimming the nest with thy brooding breast,
'Midst that young throng of future song,
    Round whom the Future sings!

THE POET OF THE WOODS

PHILOMELA

By Matthew Arnold

Hark! ah, the nightingale—
The tawny-throated!
Hark, from that moonlit cedar what a burst!
What triumph! hark!—what pain!
O wanderer from a Grecian shore,
Still, after many years, in distant lands,
Still nourishing in thy bewilder'd brain
That wild, unquench'd, deep-sunken, old-world pain—
Say, will it never heal?
And can this fragrant lawn
With its cool trees, and night,
And the sweet, tranquil Thames,
And moonshine, and the dew,
To thy rack'd heart and brain
Afford no balm?

Dost thou to-night behold,
Here, through the moonlight on this English grass,
The unfriendly palace in the Thracian wild?
Dost thou again peruse
With hot cheeks and sear'd eyes
The too clear web, and thy dumb sister's shame?
Dost thou once more assay
Thy flight, and feel come over thee,
Poor fugitive, the feathery change
Once more, and once more seem to make resound

With love and hate, triumph and agony,
Lone Daulis, and the high Cephissian vale?
Listen, Eugenia—
How thick the bursts come crowding through the leaves!
Again—thou hearest?
Eternal passion!
Eternal pain!

TO THE NIGHTINGALE

By Walter Savage Landor

Gale of the night our fathers call'd thee, bird!
   Surely not rude were they who call'd thee so,
Whether mid spring-tide mirth thy song they heard
   Or whether its soft gurgle melted woe.

They knew not, heeded not, that every clime
   Hath been attemper'd by thy minstrelsy;
They knew not, heeded not, from earliest time
   How every poet's nest was warm'd by thee.

In Paradise's unpolluted bowers
   Did Milton listen to thy freshest strain;
In his own night didst thou assuage the hours
   When Crime and Tyranny were crown'd again.

Melodious Shelley caught thy softest song,
   And they who heard his music heard not thine
Gentle and joyous, delicate and strong,
   From the far tomb his voice shall silence mine.

CHARADE: 13

By Frances Ridley Havergal

MY *first* had spread her darksome wing
O'er all the loveliness of spring;
My *third* arose with mournful wail—
The young leaves told their first sad tale,
The old oak groaned, the flowerets sighed,
The hawthorn bloom was scattered wide:
But ere my gloomy *first* had passed,
When silent was my third at last,
My *whole* awoke the moonlight dell
To list the sweet tale she could tell;
Then mingled, in strange harmony,
Silence and sweetest melody.
'Your *second*, why such strange omission?'
'Tis but a tiny preposition.

APRIL

By John Keble

LESSONS sweet of spring returning,
   Welcome to the thoughtful heart!
May I call ye sense or learning,
   Instinct pure, or heaven-taught art?
Be your title what it may,
Sweet and lengthening April day,
While with you the soul is free,
Ranging wild o'er hill and lea.

Soft as Memnon's harp at morning,
   To the inward ear devout,
Touch'd by light, with heavenly warning
   Your transporting chords ring out.
Every leaf in every nook,
Every wave in every brook,
Chanting with a solemn voice,
Minds us of our better choice.

Needs no show of mountain hoary,
   Winding shore or deepening glen,
Where the landscape in its glory
   Teaches truth to wandering men:
Give true hearts but earth and sky,
And some flowers to bloom and die, —
Homely scenes and simple views
Lowly thoughts may best infuse.

THE POET OF THE WOODS

See the soft green willow springing
   Where the waters gently pass,
Every way her free arms flinging
   O'er the moss and reedy grass.
Long ere winter blasts are fled,
See her tipp'd with vernal red,
And her kindly flower display'd
Ere her leaf can cast a shade.

Though the rudest hand assail her,
   Patiently she droops awhile,
But when showers and breezes hail her,
   Wears again her willing smile.
Thus I learn contentment's power
From the slighted willow bower,
Ready to give thanks and live
On the least that Heaven may give.

If, the quiet brooklet leaving,
   Up the stony vale I wind,
Haply half in fancy grieving
   For the shades I leave behind,
By the dusty wayside drear,
Nightingales with joyous cheer
Sing, my sadness to reprove,
Gladlier than in cultured grove.

Where the thickest boughs are twining
   Of the greenest, darkest tree,
There they plunge, the light declining —
   All may hear, but none may see.
Fearless of the passing hoof,
Hardly will they fleet aloof;
So they live in modest ways,
Trust entire, and ceaseless praise.

LYRICAL INTERLUDE: 2

By Heinrich Heine

FROM out of my tears all burning
  Many blooming flowerets break,
And all my sighs combining
  A chorus of nightingales make.

And if thou dost love me, my darling,
  To thee shall the flowerets belong;
Before thy window shall echo
  The nightingale's tuneful song.

BIANCA AMONG THE NIGHTINGALES

By Elizabeth Barrett Browning

I

The cypress stood up like a church
   That night we felt our love would hold,
And saintly moonlight seemed to search
   And wash the whole world clean as gold;
The olives crystallized the vales'
   Broad slopes until the hills grew strong:
The fire-flies and the nightingales
   Throbbed each to either, flame and song.
The nightingales, the nightingales!

II

Upon the angle of its shade
   The cypress stood, self-balanced high;
Half up, half down, as double-made,
   Along the ground, against the sky;
And we, too! from such soul-height went
   Such leaps of blood, so blindly driven,
We scarce knew if our nature meant
   Most passionate earth or intense heaven
The nightingales, the nightingales!

III

We paled with love, we shook with love,
    We kissed so close we could not vow;
Till Giulio whispered "Sweet, above
    God's Ever guaranties this Now."
And through his words the nightingales
    Drove straight and full their long clear call,
Like arrows through heroic mails,
    And love was awful in it all.
The nightingales, the nightingales!

IV

O cold white moonlight of the north,
    Refresh these pulses, quench this hell!
O coverture of death drawn forth
    Across this garden-chamber ... well!
But what have nightingales to do
    In gloomy England, called the free ...
(Yes, free to die in! . . .) when we two
    Are sundered, singing still to me?
And still they sing, the nightingales!

V

I think I hear him, how he cried
  "My own soul's life!" between their notes.
Each man has but one soul supplied,
  And that's immortal. Though his throat's
On fire with passion now, to her
  He can't say what to me he said!
And yet he moves her, they aver.
  The nightingales sing through my head,—
The nightingales, the nightingales!

VI

He says to her what moves her most.
  He would not name his soul within
Her hearing,—rather pays her cost
  With praises to her lips and chin.
Man has but one soul, 't is ordained,
  And each soul but one love, I add;
Yet souls are damned and love's profaned;
  These nightingales will sing me mad!
The nightingales, the nightingales!

NIGHTINGALES

By Charles Tennyson Turner

What spirit moves the quiring nightingales
To utter forth their notes so soft and clear?
What purport hath their music, which prevails
At midnight, thrilling all the darken'd air?
'Tis said, some weeks before the hen-birds land
Upon our shores, their tuneful mates appear;
And, in that space, by hope and sorrow spann'd,
Their sweetest melodies 'tis ours to hear;
And is it so? for solace till they meet,
Does this most perfect chorus charm the grove?
Do these wild voices, round me and above,
Of amorous forethought and condolence treat?
Well may such lays be sweetest of the sweet,
That aim to fill the intervals of Love!

THE NIGHTINGALE IN THE STUDY

By James Russell Lowell

"COME forth!" my catbird calls to me,
  "And hear me sing a cavatina
That, in this old familiar tree,
  Shall hang a garden of Alcina.

"These buttercups shall brim with wine
  Beyond all Lesbian juice or Massic;
May not New England be divine?
  My ode to ripening summer classic?

"Or, if to me you will not hark,
  By Beaver Brook a thrush is ringing
Till all the alder-coverts dark
  Seem sunshine-dappled with his singing.

"Come out beneath the unmastered sky,
  With its emancipating spaces,
And learn to sing as well as I,
  Without premeditated graces.

"What boot your many-volumed gains,
  Those withered leaves forever turning,
To win, at best, for all your pains,
  A nature mummy-wrapt in learning?

THE POET OF THE WOODS

"The leaves wherein true wisdom lies
   On living trees the sun are drinking;
Those white clouds, drowsing through the skies,
   Grew not so beautiful by thinking.

"Come out! with me the oriole cries,
   Escape the demon that pursues you!
And, hark, the cuckoo weatherwise,
   Still hiding, farther onward wooes you."

"Alas, dear friend, that, all my days,
   Has poured from that syringa thicket
The quaintly discontinuous lays
   To which I hold a season-ticket,

"A season-ticket cheaply bought
   With a dessert of pilfered berries,
And who so oft my soul hast caught
   With morn and evening voluntaries,

"Deem me not faithless, if all day
   Among my dusty books I linger,
No pipe, like thee, for June to play
   With fancy-led, half-conscious finger.

"A bird is singing in my brain
   And bubbling o'er with mingled fancies,
Gay, tragic, rapt, right heart of Spain
   Fed with the sap of old romances.

"I ask no ampler skies than those
   His magic music rears above me,
No falser friends, no truer foes,—
   And does not Dona Clara love me?

THE POET OF THE WOODS

"Cloaked shapes, a twanging of guitars,
   A rush of feet, and rapiers clashing,
Then silence deep with breathless stars,
   And overhead a white hand flashing.

"O music of all moods and climes,
   Vengeful, forgiving, sensuous, saintly,
Where still, between the Christian chimes,
   The moorish cymbal tinkles faintly!

"O life borne lightly in the hand,
   For friend or foe with grace Castilian!
O valley safe in Fancy's land,
   Not tramped to mud yet by the million!

"Bird of to-day, thy songs are stale
   To his, my singer of all weathers,
My Calderon, my nightingale,
   My Arab soul in Spanish feathers.

"Ah, friend, these singers dead so long,
   And still, God knows, in purgatory,
Give its best sweetness to all song,
   To Nature's self her better glory."

THE NIGHTINGALE'S DEATH SONG

By Felicia Dorothea Hemans

Mournfully, sing mournfully,
  And die away my heart!
The rose, the glorious rose is gone,
  And I, too, will depart.

The skies have lost their splendor,
  The waters changed their tone,
And wherefore, in the faded world,
  Should music linger on?

Where is the golden sunshine,
  And where the flower-cup's glow?
And where the joy of the dancing leaves,
  And the fountain's laughing flow?

A voice, in every whisper
  Of the wave, the bough, the air,
Comes asking for the beautiful,
  And moaning, "Where, oh! where?"

Tell of the brightness parted,
  Thou bee, thou lamb at play!
Thou lark in thy victorious mirth!
  —Are ye, too, pass'd away!

THE POET OF THE WOODS

Mournfully, sing mournfully!
   The royal rose is gone.
Melt from the woods, my spirit, melt
   In one deep farewell tone!

Not so, swell forth triumphantly,
   The full, rich, fervent strain!
Hence with young love and life I go,
   In the summer's joyous train.

With sunshine, with sweet odor,
   With every precious thing,
Upon the last warm southern breeze
   My soul its flight shall wing.

Alone I shall not linger,
   When the days of hope are past,
To watch the fall of leaf by leaf,
   To wait the rushing blast.

Triumphantly, triumphantly!
   Sing to the woods, I go!
For me, perchance, in other lands,
   The glorious rose may blow.

The sky's transparent azure,
   And the greensward's violet breath,
And the dance of light leaves in the wind,
   May these know naught of death.

No more, no more sing mournfully!
   Swell high, then break, my heart!
With love, the spirit of the wind,
   With summer I depart.

THE NIGHTINGALE AND THE ORGAN

By John Godfrey Saxe

YRIARTE

A *Nightingale* who chanced to hear
   An Organ's deep and swelling tone,
Was wont to lend a careful ear,
   That so she might improve her own.

One evening, while the Organ's note
   Thrilled through the wood, and *Philomel*
Sat tuning her melodious throat
   To imitate its wondrous swell,

A twittering *Sparrow*, hopping near,
   Said, "Prithee, now, be pleased to state
What from those wooden pipes you heat
   That you can wish to imitate?

"I do not hesitate to say,
   Whatever the stupid thing can do
To please us, in a vocal way,
   That very Organ learned from *you!*

THE POET OF THE WOODS

"Of all sweet singers none is greater
   Than *Philomel*; but, on my word!
To imitate one's imitator, —
   Can aught on earth be more absurd?"

"Nay," said the *Nightingale*, "if aught
   From me the Organ ever learned,
By him no less have I been taught,
   And thus the favor is returned.

"Thus to my singing—don't you see?
   Some needed culture I impart;
For Nature's gifts, as all agree,
   Are finest when improved by Art!"

MORAL

Whate'er the foolish *Sparrow* thought,
   The *Nightingale* (so Wisdom votes)
Was wise in choosing to be taught
   E'en by an Organ's borrowed notes.

And hence the Student may obtain
   Some useful rules to guide his course
Shun self-conceit; nor e'er disdain
   Instruction from the humblest source!

THE POET OF THE WOODS

A NIGHTINGALE IN KENSINGTON GARDENS

By Henry Austin Dobson

THEY paused,—the cripple in the chair,
   More bent with pain than age;
The mother with her lines of care;
   The many-buttoned page;

The noisy, red-cheeked nursery-maid,
   With straggling train of three;
The Frenchman with his frogs and braid;—
   All, curious, paused to see,

If possible, the small, dusk bird
   That from the almond bough
Had poured the joyous chant they heard,
   So suddenly, but now.

And one poor POET stopped and thought—
   How many a lonely lay
That bird had sung ere fortune brought
   It near the common way,

Where the crowd hears the note. And then,—
   What birds must sing the song,
To whom that hour of listening men
   Could ne'er in life belong!

But 'Art for Art!' the Poet said,
  "Tis still the Nightingale,
That sings where no men's feet will tread,
  And praise and audience fail.'

TEMA CON VARIAZONI: PRELUDE

By John Addington Symonds

I WENT a roaming through the woods alone,
And heard the nightingale that made her moan.

Hard task it were to tell how dewy-still
   Were flowers and ferns and foliage in the rays
Of Hesper, white amid the daffodil
   Of twilight fleck'd with faintest chrysoprase;
   And all the while, embower'd in leafy bays,
The bird prolong'd her sharp soul-thrilling tone.

I went a roaming through the woods alone,
And heard the nightingale that made her moan.

But as I stood and listened, on the air
   Arose another voice more clear and keen,
That startled silence with a sweet despair,
   And still'd the bird beneath her leafy screen:
   The star of Love, those lattice-boughs between,
Grew large and lean'd to listen from his zone.

I went a roaming through the woods alone,
And heard the nightingale that made her moan.

THE POET OF THE WOODS

The voice, methought, was neither man's nor boy's,
   Nor bird's nor woman's, but all these in one:
In Paradise perchance such perfect noise
   Resounds from angel choirs in unison,
   Chanting with cherubim their antiphon
To Christ and Mary on the sapphire throne.

I went a roaming through the woods alone,
And heard the nightingale that made her moan.

Then down the forest aisles there came a boy,
   Unearthly pale, with passion in his eyes;
Who sang a song whereof the sound was joy,
   But all the burden was of love that dies
   And death that lives—a song of sobs and sighs,
A wild swan's note of Death and Love in one.

I went a roaming through the woods alone,
And heard the nightingale that made her moan.

Love burn'd within his luminous eyes, and Death
   Had made his fluting voice so keen and high,
The wild wood trembled as he pass'd beneath,
   With throbbing throat singing, Love-led, to die:
   Then all was hush'd, till in the thicket nigh
The bird resum'd her sharp soul-thrilling tone.

I went a roaming through the woods alone,
And heard the nightingale that made her moan.

THE POET OF THE WOODS

But in my heart and in my brain the cry,
   The wail, the dirge, the dirge of Death and Love,
Still throbs and throbs, flute-like, and will not die,
   Piercing and clear the night-bird's tune above.—
The aching, anguish'd, wild-swan's note, whereof
The sweet sad flower of song was overblown.

I went a roaming through the woods alone,
And heard the nightingale that made her moan.

NIGHTINGALE AND CUCKOO

By Alfred Austin

O NIGHTINGALE and cuckoo! it was meet
That you should come together; for ye twain
Are emblems of the rapture and the pain
That in the April of our life compete,
Until we know not which is the more sweet,
Nor yet have learned that both of them are vain!
Yet why, O nightingale! break off thy strain,
While yet the cuckoo doth his call repeat?
Not so with me. To sweet woe die I cling
Long after echoing happiness was dead,
And so found solace. Now, alas! the sting!
Cuckoo and nightingale alike have fled;
Neither for joy nor sorrow do I sing,
And autumn silence gathers in their stead.

A COLONY OF NIGHTINGALES

By Charles Tennyson Turner

I placed the mute eggs of the Nightingale
In the warm nest, beneath a brooding thrush;
And waited long, to catch the earliest gush
Of the new wood-notes, in our northern vale;
And, as with eye and ear I push'd my search,
Their sudden music came as sweet to me,
As the first organ-tone to Holy Church,
Fresh from the Angel and St Cecily;
And, year by year, the warblers still return
From the far south, and bring us back their song,
Chanting their joy our summer groves among,
A tune the merle and goldfinch cannot learn;
While the poor thrush, that hatch'd them, listens near,
Nor knows the rival choir she settled here!

THE POET OF THE WOODS

NIGHTINGALES IN LINCOLNSHIRE

By Charles Tennyson Turner

Well I remember how the nightingale,
That linger'd in the genial South so long,
Made his sweet trespass, broke his ancient pale,
And brought into the North his wondrous song.
But, when I thought to hear his first sweet bar,
He sang a mile away: I could not seek
His chosen haunt, for I was faint and weak:
Alas! I cried, so near and yet so far:
Kind nature gathered all the sounds I love
About my window; lowings of the kine,
The thrush, the linnet, and the cooing dove;
But out, alas! how should I not repine,
When, scarce a mile beyond my garden grove,
The night-bird warbled for all ears but mine?

TO A NIGHTINGALE ON ITS RETURN

By Charles Tennyson Turner

And art thou here again, sweet nightingale,
To reproduce my happy summer mood,
When, as last year, among these shades I stood,
Or from the lattice heard thy thrilling tale?
This May-tide is but cold; yet, none the less,
I trust thy tuneful energy to sing
Through the thin leafage of this laggard spring,
With all thy blended joy and plaintiveness.
How often have my lonely steps been led,
By thy sweet voice, on to thy magic tree!
How often has thy wakeful spirit fed
My thoughts with love, and hope, and mystery!
How often hast thou made my weary head
A music chamber for my soul and thee!

THE SICK MAN
AND THE NIGHTINGALE

By Amy Levy

(From Lenau)

So late, and yet a nightingale?
Long since have dropp'd the blossoms pale,
The summer fields are ripening,
    And yet a sound of spring?

O tell me, didst thou come to hear,
Sweet Spring, that I should die this year;
And call'st across from the far shore
    To me one greeting more?

THE POET OF THE WOODS

THE NIGHTINGALE

By Katharine Tynan Hinkson

The speckled bird sings in the tree
   When all the stars are silver-pale.
Come, children, walk the night with me,
   And we shall hear the nightingale.

The nightingale is a shy bird,
   He flits before you through the night.
And now the sleepy vale is stirred
   Through all its green and gold and white.

The moon leans from her place to hear,
   The stars shed golden star-dust down,
For now comes in the sweet o' the year,
   The country's gotten the greenest gown.

The blackbird turns upon his bed,
   The thrush has oped a sleeping eye,
Quiet each downy sleepy-head;
   But who goes singing up the sky?

It is, it is the nightingale,
   In the tall tree upon the hill.
To moonlight and the dewy vale
   The nightingale will sing his fill.

THE POET OF THE WOODS

He's but a homely, speckled bird,
   But he has gotten a golden flute,
And when his wondrous song is heard,
   Blackbird and thrush and lark are mute.

Troop, children dear, out to the night,
   Clad in the moonlight silver-pale,
And in the world of green and white
   'Tis you shall hear the nightingale.

AL FAR DELLA NOTTE

By William Sharp

Hark!
As a bubbling fount
That suddenly wells
And rises in tall spiral waves and flying spray,
The high, sweet, quavering, throbbing voice
Of the nightingale!
Not yet the purple veil of dusk has fallen,
But o'er the yellow band
That binds the west
The vesper star beats like the pulse of heaven.

Up from the fields
The peasants troop
Singing their songs of love:
And oft the twang of thin string'd music breaks
High o'er the welcoming shouts,
The homing laughter.
The whirling bats are out,
And to and fro
the blue swifts wheel
Where, i' the shallows of the dusk,
The grey moths flutter
Over the pale blooms
Of the night-flowering bay.
Softly adown the slopes,
And o'er the plain,

Ave Maria
Solemnly soundeth.
The long day is over.
Dusk, and silence now:
And Night, that is as dew
On the Flower of the World.

HAST THOU HEARD THE NIGHTINGALE?

By Richard Watson Gilder

I

Yes, I have heard the nightingale.
   As in dark woods I wandered,
   And dreamed and pondered,
   A voice past by all fire
   And passion and desire;
   I rather felt than heard
   The song of that lone bird;
Yes, I have heard the nightingale.

II

Yes, I have heard the nightingale.
   I heard it, and I followed;
   The warm night swallowed
   This soul and body of mine,
   As burning thirst takes wine,
   While on and on I prest
   Close to that singing breast;
Yes, I have heard the nightingale.

III

Yes, I have heard the nightingale.
    Well doth each throbbing ember
    The flame remember;
    And I, how quick that sound
    Turned drops from a deep wound!
    How this heart was the thorn
    Which pierced that breast forlorn!
Yes, I have heard the nightingale.

NIGHTINGALES

By Robert Seymour Bridges

BEAUTIFUL must be the mountains whence ye come,
And bright in the fruitful valleys the streams, wherefrom
    Ye learn your song:
Where are those starry woods? O might I wander there,
Among the flowers, which in that heavenly air
    Bloom the year long!

Nay, barren are those mountains and spent the streams:
Our song is the voice of desire, that haunts our dreams,
    A throe of the heart,
Whose pining visions dim, forbidden hopes profound,
No dying cadence nor long sigh can sound,
    For all our art.

Alone, aloud in the raptured ear of men
We pour our dark nocturnal secret; and then,
    As night is withdrawn
From these sweet-springing meads and bursting boughs of May,
Dream, while the innumerable choir of day
    Welcome the dawn.

MY LOYAL LOVE

By Johanna Ambrosius

THE nightingale's sighing
  Mid elder leaves,
Coquetting and toying
  With soft spring breeze.
He flew to the rose,
  His love to prove:
To me ope thy chalice,
  My loyal love.

Beside garden hedge stood
  Two children fair;
They talked of a parting
  To meet elsewhere.
Weep not, little maiden,
  I'll fears disprove;
On earth thou'lt be ever
  My loyal love!

Up rises the lily
  From azure lake,
With yearning ascending
  The moon to seek.
With silvery pencil
  He writes above:
"For me live thou and die,
  My loyal love!"

THE POET OF THE WOODS

Long, long, stood I pond'ring,
   Silent, alone;
A rustling from fragrant
   Woodlands was blown.
Yet though louder growing,
   No thief did move.
His arms close, close hold me,
   My loyal love!

TO THE NIGHTINGALE (2)

By William Drummond

Dear quirister, who from those shadows sends,
Ere that the blushing dawn dare show her light,
Such sad lamenting strains that night attends
Become all ear, stars stay to hear thy plight;
If one whose grief even reach of thought transcends,
Who ne'er, not in a dream, did taste delight,
May thee importune who like case pretends
And seems to joy in woe, in woe's despite;
Tell me, so may thou Fortune milder try
And long, long sing, for what thou thus complains?
Sith, winter gone, the sun in dappled sky
Now smiles on meadows, mountains, woods and plains?
  The bird, as if my questions did her move,
    With trembling wings sobbed forth, *I love, I love.*

ECHOES: 45

By William Ernest Henley

To W. B.

From the brake the Nightingale
  Sings exulting to the Rose;
Though he sees her waxing pale
  In her passionate repose,
While she triumphs waxing frail,
  Fading even while she glows;
    Though he knows
    How it goes —
Knows of last year's Nightingale,
  Wise the well-beloved Rose!

Love and life shall still prevail,
  Nor the silence at the close
Break the magic of the tale
  In the telling, though it shows —
    Who but knows
    How it goes! —
Life a last year's Nightingale,
  Love a last year's Rose.

I. THE ROMANCER
(THREE SEVERAL BIRDS)

By James Whitcomb Riley

THE Romancer's a nightingale, —
   The moon wanes dewy-dim
And all the stars grow faint and pale
   In listening to him.—
To him the plot least plausible
   Is of the most avail,—
He simply masters it because
   He takes it by the tale.

> *O he's a nightingale,—*
>   *His theme will never fail—*
> *It gains applause of all —because*
>   *He takes it by the tale!*

The Romancer's a nightingale:—
   His is the sweetest note—
The sweetest, woe-begonest wail
   Poured out of mortal throat:
So, glad or sad, he ever draws
   Our best godspeed and hail;
He highest lifts his theme—because
   He takes it by the tale.

THE POET OF THE WOODS

O he's a nightingale,—
 His theme will never fail—
It gains applause of all—because
 He takes it by the tale!

AN ADDRESS TO THE NIGHTINGALE (FROM ARISTOPHANES)

By Agnes Mary F. Robinson

O DEAR one, with tawny wings,
Dearest of singing things,
Whose hymns my company have been,
Thou art come, thou art found, thou art seen!
Bid, with the music of thy voice,
Sweet-sounding rustler, the heart rejoice;
Ah! louder, louder, louder sing,
Flute out the language of the spring;
        Nay, let those low notes rest,
Oh! my nightingale, nightingale, carol thine anapaest!

Come, my companion, cease from thy slumbers,
Pour out thy holy and musical numbers,
Sing and lament with a sweet throat divine,
Itys of many tears, thy son and mine!
Cry out, and quiver, and shake, dusky throat,
Throb with the thrill of thy liquidest note.
Through the wide country and mournfully through
Leafy-haired branches and boughs of the yew,
Widens and rises the echo until
Even the throne-room of God it shall fill.

Then, when Apollo, the bright-locked, hath heard,
Lo, he shall answer thine elegy, bird,
Playing his ivory seven-stringed lyre,
Standing a God in the high Gods' quire.
    Ay, bird, not he alone:
  Hark! from immortal throats arise
    Diviner threnodies
That sound and swoon in a celestial moan
    And answer back thine own.

Come, my companion, cease from thy slumbers,
Pour out thy holy and musical numbers,
Sing and lament with a sweet throat divine,
Itys of many tears, thy son and mine!
Cry out, and quiver, and shake, dusky throat,
Throb with the thrill of thy liquidest note.
Through the wide country and mournfully through
Leafy-haired branches and boughs of the yew,
Widens and rises the echo, until
Even the throne-room of God it shall fill!

THE NOTIONAL NIGHTINGALE

By Amos Russel Wells

King Hubert, he went to the forest in state,
In glitter and gold, on a sunshiny day,
And commanded his train in the shadow to wait,
While a herald proclaimed in the following way:

"His Imperial Majesty, Hubert the Second,
Since the nightingale's voice is quite musical reckoned,
Is graciously pleased, as the day seems too long,
To command that the nightingale sing him a song!"

The court all stood waiting for what might befall;
But somehow, no nightingale answered the call.

THE POET OF THE WOODS

TO THE NIGHTINGALE

By Philip Ayres

Why, little charmer of the air,
 Dost thou in music spend the morn?
Whilst I thus languish in despair,
 Opprest by Cynthia's hate and scorn:
  Why does thou sing, and hear me cry;
  Tell, wanton Songster, tell me why?

I

WILT thou not cease at my desire?
Will those small organs never tire?
Nature did these close shades prepare,
Not for thy music, but my care:
Then why wilt thou persist to sing,
Thou beautiful malicious thing?
When kind Aurora first appears,
She weeps, in pity to my tears;
If thus thou think'st to give relief,
Thou never knew'st a Lover's grief.
  Then, little charmer, &c.
    That dost in music, &c.

II

Thou Feather'd Atom, where in thee
Can be compris'd such harmony?
In whose small fabric must remain,
What composition does contain.
All griefs but mine are at a stand,
When thy surprising tunes command.
How can so small a tongue and throat
Express so loud, and sweet a note?
Thou hast more various points at will,
Than Orpheus had with all his skill.
    Then, little charmer, &c.
        That dost in music, &c.

III

Great to the ear, though small to sight,
The happy Lover's dear delight,
Fly to the bow'r where such are laid,
And there bestow thy serenade.
Haste from my sorrow, haste away;
Alas, there's danger in thy stay,
Lest hearing me so oft complain,
Should make thee change thy cheerful strain,
Thy songs cannot my grief remove,
Thou harmless syren of the grove.

Then cease, thou charmer of the air,
  No more in music spend the morn,
With me that languish in despair,
  Opprest by Cynthia's hate and scorn;
    And do not this poor boon deny,
    I ask but silence whilst I die.

THE NIGHTINGALE THAT WAS DROWNED

By Philip Ayres

UPON a bough, hung trembling o'er a spring,
Sate Philomel, to respite grief, and sing:
Tuning such various notes, there seem'd to nest
A choir of little songsters in her breast,
Whilst Echo at the close of ev'ry strain,
Return'd her music, note for note again.

The jealous bird, who ne'er had rival known,
Not thinking these sweet points were all her own;
So fill'd with emulation was, that she
Express'd her utmost art and harmony;
Till as she eagerly for conquest tried,
Her shadow in the stream below she spied:

Then heard the waters bubbling, but mistook,
And thought the nymphs were laughing in the brook;
She then enrag'd, into the spring did fall,
And in sad accents thus upbraids them all:
'Not Tereus self offer'd so great a wrong,
Nymphs, take my life, since you despise my song.

TO A NIGHTINGALE HEARD UPON A HILLTOP BEFORE DAWN

By Herbert Trench

YES, Nightingale, I lie awake
And wondering hear thee sing
Over the deep world from thy brake
While every other thing
Sleepeth—the deep world like a lake
Stirred round thee, ring on ring!

More than the chanters of the light
Thy passion men confounds
Because like ours 'tis born in sight
Of that which hath no bounds:
How the dark-streaming infinite
Wells in those golden sounds!

Some traveller once in Himalay
Chanced on a tribe so lone,
So dungeoned from the world away,
They deemed it all their own,
And any human race but they
Incredible, unknown.

But up, up where the snowy crest
Of Elburz mounts the blue
And Caucasus sinks east and west
Precipitous, some few
Clansmen are found, high on its breast
Where half the earth's in view;

And these by that great prospect thrilled
Perhaps, in joy or fear,
Poor hunters wild and rudely skilled,
Have raised an altar there
"To the God Unknown"; and this they build
Of horns of goat and deer.

Like thine their dark and lofty song
Where shining gulfs expand
Beyond the Caspian — Death, Time, Wrong
That few can understand —
Is launched, and low and clear and strong
Floats out to all the land!

A RICHER FREIGHT

By William Henry Davies

You Nightingales, that came so far,
    From Afric's shore;
With these rich notes, unloaded now
    Against my door;

Most true they are far richer freight
    Than ships can hold;
That come from there with ivory tusks,
    And pearls, and gold.

But you'll return more rich, sweet birds,
    By many notes,
When you take my Love's sweeter ones
    Back in your throats,

And Afric's coast will be enriched
    By how you sing!
What! you'll bring others back with you,
    To learn—next Spring.

NIGHTINGALE LANE

By William Sharp

Down through the thicket, out of the hedges,
  A ripple of music singeth a tune . . .
    Like water that falls
    From mossy ledges
  With a soft low croon:
        Soon
   It will cease!
No, it falls but to rise —but to rise —but to rise!
It is over the thickets, it leaps in the trees,
  It swims like a star in the purple-black skies!
    Ah, once again,
    With its rapture and pain,
  The nightingale singeth under the moon!

THE CHINESE NIGHTINGALE

By Nicholas Vachel Lindsay

A Song in Chinese Tapestries

"How, how," he said. "Friend Chang," I said,
"San Francisco sleeps as the dead—
Ended license, lust and play:
Why do you iron the night away?
Your big clock speaks with a deadly sound,
With a tick and a wail till dawn comes round.
While the monster shadows glower and creep,
What can be better for man than sleep?"

"I will tell you a secret," Chang replied;
"My breast with vision is satisfied,
And I see green trees and fluttering wings,
And my deathless bird from Shanghai sings."
Then he lit five fire-crackers in a pan.
"Pop, pop," said the fire-crackers, "cra-cra-crack."
He lit a joss stick long and black.
Then the proud gray joss in the corner stirred;
On his wrist appeared a gray small bird,
And this was the song of the gray small bird:
"Where is the princess, loved forever,
Who made Chang first of the kings of men?"

THE POET OF THE WOODS

And the joss in the corner stirred again;
And the carved dog, curled in his arms, awoke,
Barked forth a smoke-cloud that whirled and broke.
It piled in a maze round the ironing-place,
And there on the snowy table wide
Stood a Chinese lady of high degree,
With a scornful, witching, tea-rose face . . .
Yet she put away all form and pride,
And laid her glimmering veil aside
With a childlike smile for Chang and for me.

The walls fell back, night was a flower,
The table gleamed in a moonlit bower,
While Chang, with a countenance carved of stone,
Ironed and ironed, all alone.
And thus she sang to the busy man Chang:
"Have you forgotten . . .
Deep in the ages, long, long ago,
I was your sweetheart, there on the sand—
Storm-worn beach of the Chinese land?
We sold our grain in the peacock town
Built on the edge of the sea-sands brown—
Built on the edge of the sea-sands brown . . .
"When all the world was drinking blood
From the skulls of men and bulls
And all the world had swords and clubs of stone,
We drank our tea in China beneath the sacred spice-trees,
And heard the curled waves of the harbor moan.
And this gray bird, in Love's first spring,
With a bright-bronze breast and a bronze-brown wing,
Captured the world with his carolling.
Do you remember, ages after,
At last the world we were born to own?
You were the heir of the yellow throne—
The world was the field of the Chinese man

And we were the pride of the Sons of Han?
We copied deep books and we carved in jade,
And wove blue silks in the mulberry shade . . . "

"I remember, I remember
That Spring came on forever,
That Spring came on forever,"
Said the Chinese nightingale.

My heart was filled with marvel and dream,
Though I saw the western street-lamps gleam,
Though dawn was bringing the western day,
Though Chang was a laundryman ironing away . . .
Mingled there with the streets and alleys,
The railroad-yard and the clock-tower bright,
Demon clouds crossed ancient valleys;
Across wide lotus-ponds of light
I marked a giant firefly's flight.

And the lady, rosy-red,
Flourished her fan, her shimmering fan,
Stretched her hand toward Chang, and said:
"Do you remember,
Ages after,
Our palace of heart-red stone?
Do you remember
The little doll-faced children
With their lanterns full of moon-fire,
That came from all the empire
Honoring the throne?—
The loveliest fête and carnival
Our world had ever known?
The sages sat about us
With their heads bowed in their beards,
With proper meditation on the sight.

THE POET OF THE WOODS

Confucius was not born;
We lived in those great days
Confucius later said were lived aright...
And this gray bird, on that day of spring,
With a bright bronze breast, and a bronze-brown wing,
Captured the world with his carolling.
Late at night his tune was spent.
Peasants,
Sages,
Children,
Homeward went,
And then the bronze bird sang for you and me.
We walked alone. Our hearts were high and free.
I had a silvery name, I had a silvery name,
I had a silvery name—do you remember
The name you cried beside the tumbling sea?"

Chang turned not to the lady slim—
He bent to his work, ironing away;
But she was arch, and knowing and glowing,
And the bird on his shoulder spoke for him.

"Darling... darling... darling... darling..."
Said the Chinese nightingale.

The great gray joss on a rustic shelf,
Rakish and shrewd, with his collar awry,
Sang impolitely, as though by himself,
Drowning with his bellowing the nightingale's cry:
"Back through a hundred, hundred years
Hear the waves as they climb the piers,
Hear the howl of the silver seas,
Hear the thunder.
Hear the gongs of holy China
How the waves and tunes combine

In a rhythmic clashing wonder,
Incantation old and fine:
   'Dragons, dragons, Chinese dragons,
   Red fire-crackers, and green fire-crackers,
   And dragons, dragons, Chinese dragons.'"

Then the lady, rosy-red,
Turned to her lover Chang and said:
"Dare you forget that turquoise dawn
When we stood in our mist-hung velvet lawn,
And worked a spell this great joss taught
Till a God of the Dragons was charmed and caught?
From the flag high over our palace home
He flew to our feet in rainbow-foam—
A king of beauty and tempest and thunder
Panting to tear our sorrows asunder.
A dragon of fair adventure and wonder.
We mounted the back of that royal slave
With thoughts of desire that were noble and grave.
We swam down the shore to the dragon-mountains,
We whirled to the peaks and the fiery fountains.
To our secret ivory house we were bourne.
We looked down the wonderful wing-filled regions
Where the dragons darted in glimmering legions.
Right by my breast the nightingale sang;
The old rhymes rang in the sunlit mist
That we this hour regain—
Song-fire for the brain.
When my hands and my hair and my feet you kissed,
When you cried for your heart's new pain,
What was my name in the dragon-mist,
In the rings of rainbowed rain?"

"Sorrow and love, glory and love,"
Said the Chinese nightingale.
"Sorrow and love, glory and love,"
Said the Chinese nightingale.

And now the joss broke in with his song:
"Dying ember, bird of Chang,
Soul of Chang, do you remember?—
Ere you returned to the shining harbor
There were pirates by ten thousand
Descended on the town
In vessels mountain-high and red and brown,
Moon-ships that climbed the storms and cut the skies.
On their prows were painted terrible bright eyes.
But I was then a wizard and a scholar and a priest;
I stood upon the sand;
With lifted hand I looked upon them
And sunk their vessels with my wizard eyes,
And the stately lacquer-gate made safe again.
Deep, deep below the bay, the sea-weed and the spray,
Embalmed in amber every pirate lies,
Embalmed in amber every pirate lies."

Then this did the noble lady say:
"Bird, do you dream of our home-coming day
When you flew like a courier on before
From the dragon-peak to our palace-door,
And we drove the steed in your singing path—
The ramping dragon of laughter and wrath:
And found our city all aglow,
And knighted this joss that decked it so?
There were golden fishes in the purple river
And silver fishes and rainbow fishes.
There were golden junks in the laughing river,
And silver junks and rainbow junks:

THE POET OF THE WOODS

There were golden lilies by the bay and river,
And silver lilies and tiger-lilies,
And tinkling wind-bells in the gardens of the town
By the black-lacquer gate
Where walked in state
The kind king Chang
And his sweet-heart mate....
With his flag-born dragon
And his crown of pearl ... and ... jade,
And his nightingale reigning in the mulberry shade,
And sailors and soldiers on the sea-sands brown,
And priests who bowed them down to your song—
By the city called Han, the peacock town,
By the city called Han, the nightingale town,
The nightingale town."

Then sang the bird, so strangely gay,
Fluttering, fluttering, ghostly and gray,
A vague, unravelling, final tune,
Like a long unwinding silk cocoon;
Sang as though for the soul of him
Who ironed away in that bower dim:—
  "I have forgotten
  Your dragons great,
  Merry and mad and friendly and bold.
Dim is your proud lost palace-gate.
I vaguely know
There were heroes of old,
Troubles more than the heart could hold,
There were wolves in the woods
Yet lambs in the fold,
Nests in the top of the almond tree ...
The evergreen tree ... and the mulberry tree ...
Life and hurry and joy forgotten,
Years on years I but half-remember ...

Man is a torch, then ashes soon,
May and June, then dead December,
Dead December, then again June.
Who shall end my dream's confusion?
Life is a loom, weaving illusion . . .
I remember, I remember
There were ghostly veils and laces . . .
In the shadowy bowery places . . .
With lovers' ardent faces
Bending to one another,
Speaking each his part.
They infinitely echo
In the red cave of my heart.
'Sweetheart, sweetheart, sweetheart.'
They said to one another.
They spoke, I think, of perils past.
They spoke, I think, of peace at last.
One thing I remember:
Spring came on forever,
Spring came on forever,"
Said the Chinese nightingale.

A NIGHTINGALE AT FRESNOY

By Jessie Belle Rittenhouse

Never, they say, were guns so loud,
   Never were flames so bright,
As those that made at Fresnoy
   Inferno of the night;

And when the searchlight fires lit
   The slender, new-green trees,
They could be seen to tremble
   As never in a breeze.

At Fresnoy, in the little wood
   Just greening with the spring,
A nightingale, undaunted,
   Lifted his voice to sing;

And in each moment's silence
   When torn earth held her breath,
Before the fearful guns again
   Uttered their Song of Death,—

The nightingale, oblivious
   Of all the ghastly strife,
Was heard within the little wood
   To sing the Song of Life!

THE SEARCH FOR THE NIGHTINGALE

By Walter James Redfern Turner

To S. S.

I

BESIDE a stony, shallow stream I sat
In a deep gully underneath a hill.
I watched the water trickle down dark moss
And shake the tiny boughs of maidenhair,
And billow on the bodies of cold stone.
And sculptured clear
Upon the shoulder of that aerial peak
Stood trees, the fragile skeletons of light,
High in a bubble blown
Of visionary stone.

II

Under that azurine transparent arch
The hill, the rocks, the trees
Were still and dreamless as the printed wood
Black on the snowy page.
It was the song of some diviner bird
Than this still country knew,
The words were twigs of burnt and blackened trees
From which there trilled a voice,
Shadowy and faint, as though it were the song
The water carolled as it flowed along.

III

Lifting my head, I gazed upon the world,
Carved in the breathless heat as in a gem,
And watched the parroquets green-feathered fly
Through crystal vacancy, and perch in trees
That glittered in a thin, blue, haze-like dream,
And the voice faded, though the water dinned
Against the stones its dimming memory.
And I ached then
To hear that song burst out upon that scene,
Startling an earth where it had never been.

IV

And then I came unto an older world.
The woods were damp, the sun
Shone in a watery mist, and soon was gone;
The trees were thick with leaves, heavy and old,
The sky was grey, and blue, and like the sea
Rolling with mists and shadowy veils of foam.
I heard the roaring of an ancient wind
Among the elms and in the tattered pines;
Lighting pale hollows in the cloud-dark sky,
A ghostly ship, the Moon, flew scudding by.

V

"O is it here," I cried, "that bird that sings
So that the traveller in his frenzy weeps?"
It was the autumn of the year, and leaves
Fell with a dizzying moan, and all the trees
Roared like the sea at my small impotent voice.
And if that bird was there it did not sing,
And I knew not its haunts, or where it went,
But carven stood and raved!
In that old wood that dripped upon my face
Upturned below, pale in its passionate chase.

VI

And years went by, and I grew slowly cold:
I had forgotten what I once had sought.
There are no passions that do not grow dim,
And like a fire imagination sinks
Into the ashes of the mind's cold grate.
And if I dreamed, I dreamed of that far land,
That coast of pearl upon a summer sea,
Whose frail trees in unruffled amber sleep
Gaudy with jewelled birds, whose feathers spray
Bright founts of colour through the tranquil day.

VII

The hill, the gully, and the stony stream
I had not thought on when this spring I sat
In a strange room with candles guttering down
Into the flickering silence. From the Moon
Among the trees still-wreathed upon the sky
There came the sudden twittering of a ghost.
And I stept out from darkness, and I saw
The great pale sky immense, transparent, filled
With boughs and mountains and wide-shining lakes
Where stillness, crying in a thin voice, breaks.

VIII

It was the voice of that imagined bird.
I saw the gully and that ancient hill,
The water trickling down from Paradise
Shaking the tiny boughs of maidenhair.
There sat the dreaming boy.
And O! I wept to see that scene again,
To read the black print on that snowy page,
I wept, and all was still.
No shadow came into that sun-steeped glen,
No sound of earth, no voice of living men.

IX

Was it a dream or was it that in me
A God awoke and gazing on his dream
Saw that dream rise and gaze into its soul,
Finding, Narcissus-like, its image there:
A Song, a transitory Shape on water blown,
Descending down the bright cascades of time,
The shadowiest-flowering, ripple-woven bloom
As ghostly as still waters' unseen foam
That lies upon the air, as that song lay
Within my heart on one far summer day?

X

Carved in the azure air white peacocks fly,
Their fanning wings stir not the crystal trees,
Bright parrots fade through dimming turquoise days,
And music scrolls its lightning calm and bright
On the pale sky where thunder cannot come.
Into that world no ship has ever sailed,
No seaman gazing with hand-shaded eyes
Has ever seen its shore whiten the waves.
But to that land the Nightingale has flown,
Leaving bright treasure on this calm air blown.

THE SONGSTERS

By William Watson

SING, Nightingale! There still be those who take
  Thy music to be sweet.
Chant thine old chant—till the new fashions make
  All melody obsolete.

I cannot doubt that soon the corncrake's note
  Shall be to thine preferred!
What then? Sing on,—with thy still golden throat,
  Still tolerated bird!

THE POET OF THE WOODS

FAIRFORD NIGHTINGALES

By John Drinkwater

THE nightingales at Fairford sing
As though it were a common thing
To make the day melodious
With tones that use to visit us
Only when thrush and blackbird take
Their sleep nor know the moon's awake.

These nightingales they sing at noon,
Not lyric lone, but threading June
With songs of many nightingales,
Till the meridian summer pales,
And here by day that spectral will
Is spending its enchantment still.

Nor shyly in far woodland bowers,
But walled among the garden flowers,
The Fairford nightingales are free,
That so the fabled melody
Is from the haunted groves of Thrace
Falling on Fairford market-place.

THE POET OF THE WOODS

O nightingales that leave the night
To join the melodists of light,
And leave your coppiced gloom to dare
The fellowship forsaken there,
Fresh hours, fresh leaves can dispossess
Nor spell your music's loneliness.

WASTED HOURS

By William Henry Davies

How many buds in this warm light
Have burst out laughing into leaves!
   And shall a day like this be gone
Before I seek the wood that holds
   The richest music known?

Too many times have nightingales
Wasted their passion on my sleep,
   And brought repentance soon:
But this one night I'll seek the woods,
   The nightingale, and moon.

THE NIGHTINGALE
NEAR THE HOUSE

By Harold Monro

Here is the soundless cypress on the lawn:
It listens, listens. Taller trees beyond
Listen. The moon at the unruffled pond
    Stares. And you sing, you sing.

That star-enchanted song falls through the air
From lawn to lawn down terraces of sound,
Darts in white arrows on the shadowed ground;
    And all the night you sing.

My dreams are flowers to which you are a bee
As all night long I listen, and my brain
Receives your song; then loses it again
    In moonlight on the lawn.

Now is your voice a marble high and white,
Then like a mist on fields of paradise,
Now is a raging fire, then is like ice,
    Then breaks, and it is dawn.

BIBLIOGRAPHY

THE NIGHTINGALE BY SIR PHILIP SIDNEY,
   First published in *Certain Sonnets*, 1598
PHILOMEL BY RICHARD BARNFIELD,
   First published in 1598.
TO THE NIGHTINGALE BY WILLIAM DRUMMOND,
   First published in *The Flowers of Sion*, 1623
ON THE DEATH OF A NIGHTINGALE
BY THOMAS RANDOLPH,
   First published in *Amyntas*, 1638
SONNET I: TO THE NIGHTINGALE BY JOHN MILTON,
   First published in *Poems of Mr. John Milton, Both English and Latin, Compos'd at leveral times*, 1645
LOVE'S NIGHTINGALE BY RICHARD CRASHAW,
   First Published in *Steps to the Temple, Sacred Poems. With the Delights of the Muses*, 1648
TO THE NIGHTINGALE
BY COUNTESS OF WINCHILSEA ANNE FINCH,
   First published in *Miscellany Poems on Several Occasions*, 1713
THE NIGHTINGALE BY JOHN VANBRUGH,
   A poem from the play *Esop; a Comedy*, 1720
THE NIGHTINGALE BY MARK AKENSIDE,
   First published under the title "Ode XV. – To the Evening Star" in *Odes on Several Subjects, Book I*, 1745
TO THE NIGHTINGALE BY JAMES THOMSON,
   First published in *The Works of James Thomson, with his Last Corrections and Improvements, Prefixed by an Account of his Life and Writing, Edited by Patrick Murdock*, 1762

AN EVENING ADDRESS TO A NIGHTINGALE
BY CUTHBERT SHAW,
> First published in *A Collection of Poems in Four Volumes. By several hands.* Vol. III. 1770

THE NIGHTINGALE AND GLOW-WORM
BY WILLIAM COWPER,
> Written in February, 1780. First published in *Poems by William Cowper, of the Inner Temple*, 1782.

INVOCATION TO THE NIGHTINGALE BY MARY HAYS,
> First published in *The Lady's Poetical Magazine, or, Beauties of British Poetry*, December 1782

ODE TO THE NIGHTINGALE
BY MARY DARBY ROBINSON,
> First published in *Poems, Volume* I, 1791

SECOND ODE TO THE NIGHTINGALE
BY MARY DARBY ROBINSON,
> First published in *Poems, Volume* I, 1791

TO THE NIGHTINGALE BY ANN RADCLIFFE,
> A poem from the novel *From the Romance of the Forest*, 1791

TO THE NIGHTINGALE, WHICH THE AUTHOR HEARD SING ON NEW YEAR'S DAY BY WILLIAM COWPER,
> First published in 1792.

TO A NIGHTINGALE BY CHARLOTTE SMITH,
> First published with the title "Sonnet III: To a Nightingale" From *Elegiac Sonnets, and Other Poems*, 1795

ON THE DEPARTURE OF THE NIGHTINGALE
BY CHARLOTTE SMITH,
> First published with the title "Sonnet VII: On the Departure of the Nightingale" From *Elegiac Sonnets, and Other Poems*, 1795

THE RETURN OF THE NIGHTINGALE
BY CHARLOTTE SMITH,
> Written in May, 1791. First published with the title "Sonnet LV. The Return of the Nightingale." From *Elegiac Sonnets, and Other Poems*, 1795

TO THE NIGHTINGALE BY ROBERT SOUTHEY,
    First published with the title "Sonnet XV.
    To the Nightingale" in *Poems, containing*
    The Restropect, Odes, Elegies, Sonnets..., *By*
    Robert Lovella and Robert Southey, 1795
THE NIGHTINGALE: A CONVERSATION POEM
BY SAMUEL TAYLOR COLERIDGE,
    First published in *Lyrical Ballads, with a Few*
    Other Poems, 1798 by William Wordsworth
THE FAIRY, THE ROSE, AND THE NIGHTINGALE;
A FABLE BY ROYALL TYLER,
    Published in *The Port Folio, New Series*, 1806
O NIGHTINGALE! THOU SURELY ART
BY WILLIAM WORDSWORTH,
    Written in 1807. First published in
    Poems of the Imagination, 1907
ODE TO A NIGHTINGALE BY JOHN KEATS,
    Written in July 1819 and first published
    in *Annals of the Fine Arts,* 1819.
THE NIGHTINGALE BY HORACE SMITH,
    First published in *Amarynthus, the Nympholept: A*
    Pastoral Drama, in Three Acts. With Other Poems, 1821
THE WOODMAN AND THE NIGHTINGALE
BY PERCY BYSSHE SHELLEY,
    Published in part by Mrs. Shelley, *Posthumous*
    Poems, 1824; the other section was published
    by Dr. Garnett, in *Relics of Shelley*, 1862.
STRADA'S NIGHTINGALE BY WILLIAM COWPER,
    Published under the title "XII. Strada's
    Nightingale" in *Minor Poems*, 1825
TO THE NIGHTINGALE
BY CHARLES TENNYSON TURNER,
    First published in *Sonnets and Fugitive Pieces*, 1830
SONG BY HARTLEY COLERIDGE,
    First published in *Poems, Songs and Sonnets,* 1833

THE NIGHTINGALE'S NEST BY JOHN CLARE,
  First published in *The Rural Muse*, 1835
THE NIGHTINGALE; CHILD'S EVENING HYMN
BY FELICIA DOROTHEA HEMANS,
  First published in *Hymns for Childhood on the Works of Nature, and Other Subjects*, 1840
TO THE NIGHTINGALE BY JOHN CLARE,
  Printed in the *English Journal*, 15th May 1841
THE NIGHTINGALE BY GEORGE LUNT,
  First Published in *Boston Miscellany of Literature and Fashion, Volume 1, January to July* 1842. Edited by Nathan Hale. Reprinted in *Lyric Poems, Sonnets and Miscellanies*, 1854
TO THE NIGHTINGALE BY FRANCES ANNE KEMBLE,
  First published in *Poems*, 1844
EASTERN SUNSET BY FRANCES ANNE KEMBLE,
  First published in *Poems*, 1844
TO A NIGHTINGALE BY GEORGE MEREDITH,
  First published in *Poems*, 1851
PHILOMELA BY MATTHEW ARNOLD,
  First published *Sohrab and Rustum: and Other Poems*, 1853
TO THE NIGHTINGALE BY WALTER SAVAGE LANDOR,
  First published under the title "CLXXIX – To the Nightingale" in *The Last Fruit Off an Old Tree*, 1853
CHARADE: 13 BY FRANCES RIDLEY HAVERGAL,
  Written in 1858. First published in *Life Echoes*, 1883
APRIL BY JOHN KEBLE,
  First published under the title "First Day After Epiphany." in *The Christian Year*, 1860
LYRICAL INTERLUDE: 2 BY HEINRICH HEINE,
  Published under the title "II. Lyrical Interlude – 1822-23, Prologue – 2." in *The Poems of Heine*, 1861, Edited by Edgar Alfred Bowring

BIANCA AMONG THE NIGHTINGALES
BY ELIZABETH BARRETT BROWNING,
   First published in *Last Poems*, 1862
NIGHTINGALES BY CHARLES TENNYSON TURNER,
   First published in *Sonnets*, 1864
THE NIGHTINGALE IN THE STUDY
BY JAMES RUSSELL LOWELL,
   First published in *Under the Willows*, 1869
THE NIGHTINGALE'S DEATH SONG
BY FELICIA DOROTHEA HEMANS,
   Published in *The Poems of Felicia Hemans*, 1875
THE NIGHTINGALE AND THE ORGAN
BY JOHN GODFREY SAXE,
   First published in *Leisure-day Rhymes*, 1875
A NIGHTINGALE IN KENSINGTON GARDENS
BY HENRY AUSTIN DOBSON,
   First published in *Proverbs in Porcelain,*
   and Other Verses, 1877
TEMA CON VARIAZONI: PRELUDE
BY JOHN ADDINGTON SYMONDS,
   First published in *Many Moods, A Volume of Verse*, 1878
NIGHTINGALE AND CUCKOO BY ALFRED AUSTIN,
   First published in *Soliloquies in Song*, 1882
A COLONY OF NIGHTINGALES
BY CHARLES TENNYSON TURNER,
   First published under the title "CCLXXVIL – A Colony of
   Nightingales" in *Collected Sonnets, Old and New*, 1884
NIGHTINGALES IN LINCOLNSHIRE
BY CHARLES TENNYSON TURNER ,
   First published under the title "CCCXXVII – Nightingales
   in Lincolnshire" in *Collected Sonnets, Old and New*, 1884
TO A NIGHTINGALE ON ITS RETURN
BY CHARLES TENNYSON TURNER,
   First published under the title "CCCXIII" in
   Collected Sonnets, Old and New, 1884

THE SICK MAN AND THE NIGHTINGALE BY AMY LEVY,
   First published in *A Minor Poet and Other Verse*, 1884
THE NIGHTINGALE BY KATHARINE TYNAN HINKSON,
   First published in *Ballads and Lyrics*, 1891
AL FAR DELLA NOTTE BY WILLIAM SHARP,
   First published in *Flower o' the Vine*, 1892
HAST THOU HEARD THE NIGHTINGALE?
BY RICHARD WATSON GILDER,
   The Great Remembrance, and Other Poems, 1893
NIGHTINGALES BY ROBERT SEYMOUR BRIDGES,
   Appears in *The Shorter Poems of Robert Bridges,* in *Book* V, first published 1893.
MY LOYAL LOVE BY JOHANNA AMBROSIUS,
   First published in *Johanna Ambrosius, a German Folk Poet. Poems*, 1894
TO THE NIGHTINGALE (2) BY WILLIAM DRUMMOND,
   Published under the title " Sonnet XXV" in *The Poems of William Drummond of Hawthornden*, 1894, Edited by William C. Ward
ECHOES: 45 BY WILLIAM ERNEST HENLEY,
   First published in *Poems*, 1898
I. THE ROMANCER (THREE SEVERAL BIRDS)
BY JAMES WHITCOMB RILEY,
   First published in *The Flying Islands of the Night*, 1900
AN ADDRESS TO THE NIGHTINGALE
(FROM ARISTOPHANES) BY AGNES MARY F. ROBINSON,
   First published in *Collected Poems, Lyrical and Narrative*, 1902
THE NOTIONAL NIGHTINGALE
BY AMOS RUSSEL WELLS,
   First published in *Rollicking Rhymes for Youngsters*, 1902
TO THE NIGHTINGALE BY PHILIP AYRES,
   Published in *Minor Poets of the Caroline Period*, 1905 By George Saintsbury

THE HAPPY NIGHTINGALE BY PHILIP AYRES,
   Published in *Minor Poets of the Caroline
   Period,* 1905 By George Saintsbury
THE NIGHTINGALE THAT WAS DROWNED
BY PHILIP AYRES,
   Published in *Minor Poets of the Caroline
   Period,* 1905 By George Saintsbury
TO A NIGHTINGALE HEARD
UPON A HILLTOP BEFORE DAWN
BY HERBERT TRENCH,
   First published in *New Poems,* 1907
A RICHER FREIGHT BY WILLIAM HENRY DAVIES,
   First published in *Nature Poems,* 1908
NIGHTINGALE LANE BY WILLIAM SHARP,
   First published in *Songs and Poems, Old and New,* 1909
THE CHINESE NIGHTINGALE
BY NICHOLAS VACHEL LINDSAY,
   First published in *The Chinese Nightingale
   and Other Poems,* 1915
A NIGHTINGALE AT FRESNOY
BY JESSIE BELLE RITTENHOUSE,
   First published in *The Door of Dreams,* 1918
THE SEARCH FOR THE NIGHTINGALE
BY WALTER JAMES REDFERN TURNER,
   First published in *The Dark Wind,* 1920
THE SONGSTERS BY WILLIAM WATSON,
   Written in 1920. Published in *Selected
   Poems of Sir William Watson,* 1928
FAIRFORD NIGHTINGALES BY JOHN DRINKWATER,
   First published in *Seeds of Time,* 1921
WASTED HOURS BY WILLIAM HENRY DAVIES,
   First published in *The Hour of Magic and Other Poems,* 1922
THE NIGHTINGALE NEAR THE HOUSE
BY HAROLD MONRO,
   First published in *Real Property,* 1922